introduction
to
modern
sheet metal

introduction to modern sheet metal

EDWARD R. KRATFEL

Scientific Research Instruments
Subsidiary of G.D. Searle
   Baltimore, Maryland

*Membership: American Society of Metals
            Instrument Society of America*

RESTON PUBLISHING COMPANY, INC.
Reston, Virginia
A Prentice-Hall Company

Library of Congress Cataloging in Publication Data

Kratfel, Edward R
  Introduction to modern sheet metal.

  Includes index.
  1. Sheet-metal work.   I. Title.
TS250.K75   671   75–35738
ISBN 0–87909–395–1

10   9   8   7   6   5   4   3   2   1

Printed in the United States of America.

*This book is dedicated to
my family and the many
friends whose advice and help
led to its completion.*

contents

preface

The sheet metal technician of today is called upon to create and produce a wide range of metal products. This range includes artistic, prototype, and production items.

In the performance of this skill, the individual must possess a basic knowledge much like that of an artist. This is to say that he must have a basic knowledge of the procedures, tools, and processes that make up the final product.

Introduction to Modern Sheet Metal is thus presented in a *graded level* so that a total exposure for the beginner is achieved.

Chapters 1 and 2 provide the student with a full understanding of metals—applications, makeup, and physical characteristics.

Chapter 3 discusses a basic set of hand tools used to lay out and to produce some of the more simple operations in sheet metal.

To better prepare the student for his work role, *precision* layout is defined, discussed, and illustrated in Chapter 4. Bend radii calculations and tables, as well as stretchout patterns, are presented.

Chapters 5 and 6 describe the basic forming tools used to work on larger work projects encountered both in the school shop and in industry. These chapters cover shearing, bending, roll forming, and punching.

A clear description of the techniques of *joints, fasteners,* and *bonding* is discussed in Chapters 7 and 8. The present techniques, including *dip brazing,* are put forth.

The important subject of metal finishing is discussed in Chapter 9. Graining, painting, irriditing, plating, and anodizing are detailed.

Sheet metal parts produced by die forming and spinning tools are discussed for the general knowledge of the student in Chapter 10. Simple examples are shown to aid in the understanding of these processes.

For the person whose direction is purely artistic, a chapter in the free forming of sheet metal is included.

For all, a project section is included at the end of this text. It is hoped that the projects will both develop the basic techniques put forth in this text and stimulate the interest of the student.

Edward R. Kratfel

1

metals

[1-1]
introduction

As a beginning student in the metal trades, this is in all probability your first encounter with the types and forms of the products that you will encounter both in school and in industrial shops.

A variety of specific metals are in common use, each with specific characteristics that lend themselves well to various work applications. Selection of a particular metal is generally governed by two important factors: *ease of workability* and the *environment in which the part is to exist*.

When we talk of workability, we are talking of the metal's ability to be sheared, bent, formed, punched, welded, or painted, or to conform to various other operations.

The purpose of this chapter is to discuss some basic definitions used to describe a metal's physical characteristics. Specific metals will then be presented in Chapter 2. Makeup, physical characteristics, and workability of each will be discussed.

[1-2]
basic definitions

Metal is a term used generally to describe a whole family of specific materials. A pure chemistry definition: *Metals are those elements that, when dissolved in a weak acid solution, carry a positive charge and are attracted by the negative pole in an electric cell.* The only nonmetallic element that is an exception to the above definition is hydrogen.

For a more understandable definition, let us assign and define a set of more basic observations of a metal.

Metals generally have a silvery or shiny color. In most cases they conduct both heat and electricity. Most metals are *malleable;* that is, they can be beaten into thin sheets by hammering or rolling. Another important property of metal is that it is *ductile.* Ductility is a term used to describe the metal's ability to be reduced in diameter or size by forcing it through a die or hole that is smaller than the original size of the rod.

The above general description of metallic properties holds true for the more commonly used metals that you will encounter. There are some metals that do not possess the properties of being malleable and ductile— calcium is an example.

Table 1-1 is a list of what are called *basic metals* that exist and are refined in our world. *Basic metals are considered pure in that they are composed of only one element.* During man's existence, however, he has found that blending one or more of the basic metals together achieves an end product that better meets his needs. Thus alloys are created. *An alloy is defined as a mixture of two or more basic metals. Alloys are formed so as to achieve a desired end result.* Most, if not all, of today's common metal products are classified as alloys. Lead, tin, and copper, however, are basic metals; most aluminum products are alloys.

Metals, be they pure or alloy, can be further defined as being *ferrous* or *nonferrous* in makeup. Any metal that is composed of iron or alloyed with iron is defined as a *ferrous metal.* Any metal or alloy not composed of iron or partly of iron is defined as *nonferrous.*

Table 1-1
METALS—WEIGHTS
AND MELTING POINTS

Metal or composition	Weight per cubic inch, pound	Weight per cubic foot, pounds	Melting point, deg. F.
Aluminum	0.0975	168.5	1220
Antimony	0.2390	413.0	1167
Barium	0.1365	235.9	1562
Bismuth	0.3532	610.3	520
Boron	0.0916	158.2	4172
Brass: 80C., 20Z.	0.3105	536.6	1823
70C., 30Z.	0.3048	526.7	1706
60C., 40Z.	0.3018	521.7	1652
50C., 50Z.	0.2961	511.7	1616
Bronze: 90C., 10T.	0.3171	547.9	1841
Cadmium	0.3123	539.6	610
Calcium	0.0556	96.1	1490
Chromium	0.2502	432.4	2939
Cobalt	0.3145	543.5	2696
Copper	0.3210	554.7	1981
Gold	0.6969	1204.3	1945
Iridium	0.8096	1399.0	4262
Iron, cast	0.254-0.279	438.7-482.4	1990-2300
Iron, wrought	0.282-0.285	486.7-493.0	2750
Lead	0.4096	707.7	621
Magnesium	0.0628	108.6	1204
Manganese	0.2636	455.5	2300
Mercury (68°F.)	0.4892	845.3	-38
Molybdenum	0.3683	636.5	4748
Nickel	0.3178	549.1	2651
Platinum	0.7717	1333.5	3224
Potassium	0.0314	54.3	144
Silver	0.376-0.380	650.2-657.1	1761
Sodium	0.0351	60.6	207
Steel, Carbon	0.283-0.284	489.0-490.8	2500
Tantalum	0.5998	1035.8	5162
Tellurium	0.2257	390.0	846
Tin	0.2633	454.9	449
Titanium	0.1621	280.1	3272
Tungsten	0.672-0.690	1161-1192	6098
Uranium	0.6753	1166.9	< 3362
Vanadium	0.2022	349.4	3110
Zinc	0.254-0.259	439.3-446.8	788

Another term used to define a metallic classification is magnetic or paramagnetic. *Magnetic metal is any metal or alloy that is drawn to a magnet. A paramagnetic metal is that which is not drawn by a magnet.* Some common examples of paramagnetic metals include lead, brass, aluminum, copper, tin, silver, and gold. Pure nickel, often used in electrical circuits, is slightly magnetic at room temperature but loses its magnetic tendency at higher temperatures.

A general rule of thumb is that ferrous metals are magnetic in nature.

[1-3]
melting temperatures

The melting temperature of a metal, be it basic or an alloy, is of extreme importance in selecting a particular metal for some specific application.

The melting temperature of a metal is that temperature at which the metal turns to a fluid state.

Sprinkler systems, used to protect industrial or commercial areas, very often make use of low-temperature alloys to operate the water spray. One particular alloy, sometimes called ''Wood's metal,'' is used to seal water from the sprinkler head. The melting temperature of this metal alloy can be selected between 140°F to 212°F. Thus, when the heat of a fire reaches 140°F or higher, the low-temperature seal melts and allows water to spray onto the burning area.

At the high end of the melting scale, a product generally called *stainless steel* is used. Stainless steel products find frequent use in environments where temperatures are high and strength of the material is important.

Table 1-1 includes a list of melting temperatures of most of the commonly used metal products.

When selecting a metal to operate in a heated environment, you should always try to select one that has a melting temperature of approximately three times its environment. Most metals go through a *plastic* state as they approach their melting temperature. These *plastic* states are temperature levels at which the metal starts to *creep* or *sag* under its own weight, thus losing its ability to maintain its shape, strength, or form.

[1-4]
corrosion

Practically all metals in common use today, with some exceptions, are corroded in one way or another. Corrosion, as applied to metals, is a chemical reaction of the metal itself with some chemical or combination of chemicals with the end effect of producing an oxide film on the metal or the destruction of the metal product itself.

The two most common chemical agents that react with metals are *air* and *water*. Air, which contains oxygen, is a very active oxidizer with most metals.

Ordinary steel and its products, exposed to both air and water, will exhibit the corrosive state commonly called *"rusting."* *Rusting* is a name reserved for cast iron or steel and its alloys where a characteristic reddish brown film of oxide forms on the surface of the metal. If left unchecked the oxidation proceeds until there is none of the original metal left, and in its place is only an *oxide of the metal.*

Copper that has been exposed to a combination of air and water will also corrode. This corrosion takes the form of a greenish film that develops on the surface.

There is a group of metals in which the process of corroding stops after an oxide film has been developed. The reason for this halt is that the film acts as a protective barrier against both air and water. Copper, as previously mentioned, exhibits this characteristic and finds frequent use as flashings, downspouts, and coverings on building roofs. Aluminum is another metal whose initial oxide coat stops the further process of oxidation.

In our modern world of today, we are asked to expose various metals to a whole range of potentially corrosive elements other than air or water. The chemical industry, particularly, makes large demands for nonreacting metals. Acids, oxidizers, and caustic solutions such as lye are by and large carried by metal products that must not react with the particular chemical or compound. The food packaging industry must also use metals that do not react or corrode with the food with which they are in contact. This is of extreme importance, as eating food products that contain oxides of metals can be hazardous to health.

In summary, the environment in which a particular metal is to exist plays an important part in its selection. You must ask the question, "What will this metal be exposed to?"

Coatings applied to the basic metal product, such as paint or a metal plating, can protect the basic metal from corrosion. This will be discussed in Chapter 9, "Sheet Metal Finishing."

To aid in both present and future selections of metal products, Table 1-2 gives the various operating environments of some common metals and alloys.

Table 1-2
GOOD—FAIR—POOR

	Heat	ENVIRONMENTS *Air–Water*	*Acid*	*Base*
Aluminum	G	G	F	P
Brass	G	G	F	F
Copper	G	G	F	F
Hot rolled steel	G	F→P	F	F
Cold rolled steel	G	P	F	F
Galvanized steel	F	G	P	P
Nickel	G	G	G	G
Stainless steel	G	G	G	G
Lead	P	G	G	G
Gold	G	G	G	G
Silver	F	F	P	P
Tin	P	G	F	F
Chrome (plate)	F	G	G	G
Cadmium (plate)	F	G	F→P	F→P

[1-5]
workability-hardness

The word *workability*, as applied to the various metal products, is a general term that contains several important facts about any particular metal. These facts can be listed as hardness, machinability, forming and bending, welding or bonding, and the ability to be punched (as to produce a hole).

Let us discuss the *hardness* of a metal and pursue it to a simple understanding.

Generally, the hardness of a metal can be said to lie within three general categories: *soft, tempered,* or *hardened.* Each of these three states is produced not by mere change, but by special processes employed by the manufacturers of the particular metal product. There are some metals, such as lead and tin, that exist in one state, the soft state, and cannot be reworked or processed so that they will approach the temper or hardened state.

A *soft metal,* often said to be in the *annealed state,* is generally produced by specially heat treating the metal product. The heating process has the effect of producing a poor strength bond between the material's molecules.

Soft metals can be generally determined by a simple field test. The point of a pocket knife or some other such hard metal object dragged across the metal will leave a deep ragged scratch. In some cases, such as copper, soft spinners or shavings can be produced by the above test. Another test of a metal's softness is its ability to produce a permanent bend. This is to say that a round bar or sheet of a soft state metal can be bent with light to moderate pressure. When the pressure is removed, the shape of the bend is retained by the metal with no tendency on its part to return to its original or near original shape prior to the bending pressure.

Annealed metals are important, and this *soft* feature is employed in the formation of many important shapes and forms in the metal trades, where a harder state would prove difficult to work. All of the general metal products that you, the technician, will encounter can be obtained in the annealed or soft state. Here again the final use and purpose of the product will be specified or known.

The tempered state, sometimes called the *spring* state, is a condition imparted to the metal product by both a rolling process and a heating process. You will remember that in the soft state, the molecules of the metal do not resist the tendency to bend or pull away from one another. The tempered state, however, is one in which the resistance to bending or pulling is increased by "packing" the molecules closer together.

The old-time blacksmith did a tempering process to a variety of tools and plows by a heating, beating, and water quenching process. He may not have known it, but he was compacting the very molecules of his metal piece, making it stronger and tempered.

Tempered metals can be *field tested* in much the same way as soft metals. The scratch test will still produce a scratch, except that the mark left is generally smooth and shallow. A spinner produced from this scratch test will be curled and springlike. Bending a piece of tempered metal is more difficult than bending a soft metal. When mild pressure is applied to the tempered piece and released, you will notice that the material will *spring* back to its original shape. As more and more pressure is applied, you will reach a point where the molecular bond strength is breached, and the metal will retain a permanent bend. When the pressure is released, the bent portion will move slightly towards its original condition. Some degrees of temper are such that when the metal is sharply bent, an actual crack is produced along the bend line. A crack so produced renders the metal part of no use.

Here, as with soft or annealed metals, many of the commonly encountered metal products can be obtained in varying degrees of temper.

The hardened state of metals is possibly the narrowest group of metals that you will be asked to perform operations upon. The basic principle of metal working, whether it be machining or sheet metal, is that the cutting or forming tool be of a harder nature than the material on which it is working. A truly hardened metal will fail the scratch test, in that no scratch is produced. Some bending of the metal piece can be achieved, but as pressure is increased, the metal piece will break completely apart. Very highly hardened material will not even allow itself to be scratched with a hardened metal file.

Common hardened metals fall generally into two ferrous metal groups, carbon steel and stainless steels.

In summary, both machinability and forming of a metal relate to its particular state of hardness. As to machinability or that process where metal is removed by a cutting tool or edge, the following rule of thumb can be applied. Metals with a range of soft to temper will machine with an easy to moderate tool pressure. Hardened metals generally are cut with abrasive wheels or carbide-tipped cutting tools. General shop tools will not prove effective in machining these "hard" metals.

From our previous discussion on the "molecule strength" of each hardness state, we found that forming the soft or annealed material is the best selection, whereas temper through hard will prove somewhat difficult to impossible to form.

review questions

1-1 / What exactly does the term workability mean to you when discussing metal products?

1-2 / Define *basic metals* and alloys. Give several examples of each.

1-3 / Which of the following metals are ferrous in nature: iron, silver, bronze, nickel, steel, stainless steel, aluminum?

1-4 / What are the various stages that a metal passes through from its solid state as its temperature is increased? Why is this important in metal selection?

1-5 / Some metals exhibit a characteristic that prevents their oxidation from water and air. Describe this process and give examples.

1-6 / List the three states of hardness for metals. Describe a simple test for each, and give at least two examples for each state.

1-7 / On a drawing detailing a metal tank, the designer has specified that tin-plated steel is to be used in its fabrication. To make the seams tight, tin solder is used. This tank is to operate in an oven heated to approximately 850° F. What are your thoughts on this tank?

1-8 / What is the basic requirement of tools used to form or cut metal?

1-9 / In the food industry, what is a prime consideration in selecting metal products that are in contact with food?

1-10 / How would you define *pure nickel:* magnetic or nonmagnetic?

1-11 / Four blocks of metal, each having a volume of one cubic foot, are sitting on the floor. They are painted entirely black and have only a weight value assigned to each. Block A weighs 547 lbs; block B, 554 lbs; block C, 549 lbs; and block D, 454 lbs. Identify the metal that each block is made of.

1-12 / List some of the methods used to eliminate corrosion on common steel products.

1-13 / Can all metals in a soft hardness state be worked or changed to the temper or hardened state?

1-14 / List a simple kit of items or tools that could be used to determine whether a material is a metal or a nonmetal.

1-15 / As a sheet metal technician, what single most important factor should you know about a metal product before working it into a required form?

2

metals
and their
properties

[2-1]
introduction

This chapter is designed to help you as you select and work with the general types of metals employed in the industry. We begin with a discussion of the various forms, grades, and finishes of metal products in common use. The "gauge" system of sizing a sheet thickness and wire diameter will be discussed.

The latter section of the chapter specifically lists properties of the more commonly used metals. This portion of the chapter is intended as an aid in the selection and evaluation of present and future sheet metal projects.

[2-2]

manufactured forms and grades

The methods used by the metal industry to create various products are essentially the same in most cases.

The particular metal, be it basic or alloy, is initially refined or alloyed to exacting standards. This initial process is performed in a blast furnace, an open hearth, or an electric furnace. These furnaces create the basic metal or alloy mixture of the metal. From the furnace, the metal is cast into some form for further processing and forming.

The next step in this process is the forming of the casting into various forms such as round rods, square or rectangular bars, sheets, or other useful forms. This forming, in almost all cases, makes use of a rolling mill. The cylindrical rolls of a mill (driven by powerful motor drives) can produce a variety of shapes, depending on the forms on the rolls (see Fig. 2-1).

The metal product to be formed by the rolling mills may be in either a cold state or highly heated state prior to the operation. Steel and most of its alloys are heated to very high temperatures to allow the rolls to squeeze and form the material without undue pressure being put on the rolls. Aluminum, however, can generally be rolled to its desired shape at room temperature. Metal products can thus be specified as *hot rolled* or *cold rolled,* and the difference in their surface finish is quite different.

[2-3]

hot rolled products

In the hot rolled process, a metal is in a red to orange glowing heated state. Under this condition of heat, and in the presence of air and moisture, oxidation or corrosion begins at a rapid pace. Even as the metal is rolled and formed, the oxide coating, sometimes called *scale,* is ever reforming.

As the rolls pass over the metal and scale, the very hard layer of scale is pressed into the metal surface below it and forms a somewhat pitted and rough surface.

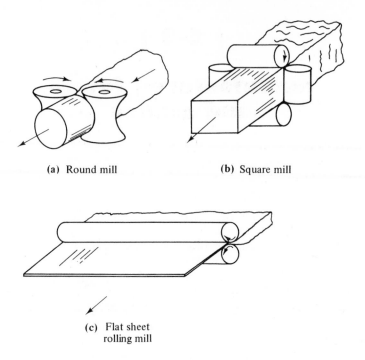

(a) Round mill **(b)** Square mill

(c) Flat sheet rolling mill

Figure 2-1 — Milled forms.

After forming, the finished metal product is allowed to cool with its hard oxide coating still covering its exterior surfaces. To remove this oxide scale and thus expose the metal surface below it, a process called *pickling* is performed. Pickling generally is a water-acid solution that is stored in large open tanks. The cooled metal products are submerged in the solution, which removes the oxide film. The cleaned metal product, however, still bears the scars of the oxide scale it developed in the heating and forming process. The surface generally looks as if it has been formed by fine to medium grains of sand.

[2-4]
cold rolled products

When metal products must be accurate in size and must possess a smooth flawless surface, the cold rolling process is used. This process uses a metal shape whose sizes are slightly larger than those of the final product. The primary metal may be of either a hot or cold rolled nature. The rolls in this process are accurately controllable as to the thickness of the metal product formed by them. The absence of heat has the effect of not producing an oxide coating during the rolling; in some cases, a fine spray of oil is used to protect the cold rolled finish.

As the metal is fed into the highly polished rolls that are set at accurate distances from one another, the metal is *sized* by the distance between the rolls and also has a smooth clean surface finish imparted to it.

Metal products formed by cold rolling can possess a size or thickness accuracy within 0.001 to 0.005 inch. The range of cold rolled products includes plates, sheets, round rod, square and rectangular bars, tubing, angles, hexagon-shaped bars, and others.

[2-5]
extruded products

In Chapter 1, we discussed the term *ductile* and defined ductility as that property of a metal that allows it to be reduced in diameter or size by forcing it through a die or hole that is smaller than the original size of the metal. Many metal products such as wire, tube, pipe, angles, and special shapes are formed by the *extrusion process*. Metal products that are not very ductile in nature can be made to approximate that condition by heating them to their "plastic" state.

Let us consider for a moment the simple extrusion of a small round rod (wire) of, say, ⅛-inch diameter (0.125 in.). Figure 2-2 shows the simplified setup of the extrusion press.

The extrusion press consists essentially of three main parts: ram cylinder, ram, and die plate. The ram cylinder is a hollow round cylinder of sufficient length to allow both a metal slug to be inserted and the head of a ram. The ram is a shaft fitted with a cylindrical head that slides within the cylinder bore. A pushing force is supplied to the ram with

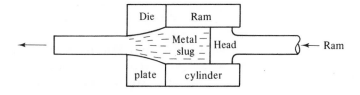

Figure 2-2 — Extrusion.

either hydraulic or screw thread pressure. The die plate is a hardened and polished end cap secured to the exit end of the ram cylinder. The die plate contains the size and shape of the finished part.

A ductile or "plastic state" metal slug is inserted between the die plate and ram head. Pressure is then supplied to the ram sufficiently to cause the metal slug material to squeeze or extrude through the hole in the die plate. Extruded products exhibit both excellent sizing and surface finishes in the end product.

Aluminum, copper, brass, and steel are often used to produce a variety of shapes and forms by the extrusion process.

[2-6]
available shapes and sizes

It is most important for the technician to be aware of the various shapes of metal products available for his use. The general list of shapes includes plate, round bars, square bars, rectangular bars, angles, hexagonal and octagonal bars, tubing, pipe, sheets, and coiled strips.

With the exceptions of pipe, wire, and sheet sizes, each of the above shapes can be ordered by giving their physical size measurements. Table 2-1 is included as a guide for specifying particular shapes and sizes.

[2-7]
pipe

Pipe, as its name implies, is used to carry gas, liquids, steam, and other products from one source to another, be it the pipe that carries water from a reservoir to your home, or an oil pipeline that carries crude or refined oil over great distances.

Commercial pipe is produced by two main processes; the products are called *seam welded pipe* and *seamless extruded pipe*.

Pipe, as produced by the various mills, can be obtained in a *size* range that generally begins with ⅛-inch pipe and proceeds to a 24-inch pipe. Table 2-2 shows the pipe sizes with their actual outside diameter measurements. Depending on use and pressure requirements, three wall thicknesses are available. An increase of wall thickness within a specific

Table 2-1
SHAPES

Shape		Necessary dimensions to order
●	Wire	Gauge or diameter
● *D*	Rod	Diameter (*D*)
S ■	Square	Length (*S*) of one side
W *T* ▬	Rectangle	Width (*W*) and thickness (*T*)
A.F. ⬡	Hexagon	Distance across the flats (*A.F.*)
H *T* *W* ◣	Angle	Outside width (*W*) × outside height (*H*) × thickness (*T*)
T ○ *D*	Tubing	Diameter (*D*) × wall thickness (*T*)
◯	Pipe	Pipe size × standard or heavy wall
W *H* □ *T*	Box tubing	Width (*W*) × height (*H*) × wall thickness (*T*)
T *H* *W* ⊔	Channel	Width (*W*) × height (*H*) × thickness (*T*)
T *W* ▬	Sheet	Thickness (*T*) gauge or decimal × width (*W*)
T *W* ▬	Plate	Thickness (*T*) fractional × width

pipe size does not affect the outside diameter of the pipe—merely its bore or hole size.

Table 2-2
STANDARD PIPE SIZES

NOMINAL PIPE SIZE	OUTSIDE DIAMETER OF PIPE	THREADS PER INCH
1/16	0.3125	27
1/8	0.405	27
1/4	0.540	18
3/8	0.675	18
1/2	0.840	14
3/4	1.050	14
1	1.315	11½
1¼	1.660	11½
1½	1.900	11½
2	2.375	11½

[2-8]
sheet and wire gauge

Being a technician in the metal trade, you should now become familiar with the meaning and use of "gauge sizes" in dealing with both wire and sheet sizes. A gauge size is merely a method of specifying the diameter of a wire or the thickness of a sheet by a gauge number, where its size does not exactly equal a fractional part of an inch. This system was born to facilitate identification of the vast range of products, whether round or sheet.

The gauge system merely assigns a number called the *sheet or wire gauge size* to specify its actual decimal size. Table 2-3 lists four systems used by the United States and the United Kingdom.

The *American* or *Brown and Sharpe* system is used for all wire metal products except steel and iron. *The American Steel and Wire Co.* or *Washburn and Moen gauge* sizes are used exclusively for steel and iron products. The *imperial* wire gauge sizes are used officially by the United Kingdom.

Measurement of both wire gauge or sheet gauge sizes is performed with the aid of two measuring tools: a wire gauge or a 0-to-1-inch outside micrometer. These tools will be discussed in Chapter 3. To determine the

Table 2-3A
WIRE GAUGES IN APPROXIMATE
DECIMALS OF AN INCH

No. of wire gauge	American wire or Brown & Sharpe gauge	Steel wire gauge (U.S.)*	British standard wire gauge (Imperial wire gauge)	Music or piano wire gauge	Birmingham or Stub's iron wire gauge	Stub's steel wire gauge	No. of wire gauge	Stub's steel wire gauge
7/0	. . .	0.4900	0.5000	. . .	. . .	. . .	51	0.066
6/0	0.5800	0.4615	0.4640	0.004	. . .	. . .	52	0.063
5/0	0.5165	0.4305	0.4320	0.005	0.5000	. . . .	53	0.058
4/0	0.4600	0.3938	0.4000	0.006	0.4540	. . .	54	0.055
3/0	0.4096	0.3625	0.3720	0.007	0.4250	. . .	55	0.050
2/0	0.3648	0.3310	0.3480	0.008	0.3800	. . .	56	0.045
1/0	0.3249	0.3065	0.3240	0.009	0.3400	. . .	57	0.042
1	0.2893	0.2830	0.3000	0.010	0.3000	0.227	58	0.041
2	0.2576	0.2625	0.2760	0.011	0.2840	0.219	59	0.040
3	0.2294	0.2437	0.2520	0.012	0.2590	0.212	60	0.039
4	0.2043	0.2253	0.2320	0.013	0.2380	0.207	61	0.038
5	0.1819	0.2070	0.2120	0.014	0.2200	0.204	62	0.037
6	0.1620	0.1920	0.1920	0.016	0.2030	0.201	63	0.036
7	0.1443	0.1770	0.1760	0.018	0.1800	0.199	64	0.035
8	0.1285	0.1620	0.1600	0.020	0.1650	0.197	65	0.033
9	0.1144	0.1483	0.1440	0.022	0.1480	0.194	66	0.032
10	0.1019	0.1350	0.1280	0.024	0.1340	0.191	67	0.031
11	0.0907	0.1205	0.1160	0.026	0.1200	0.188	68	0.030
12	0.0808	0.1055	0.1040	0.029	0.1090	0.185	69	0.029
13	0.0720	0.0915	0.0920	0.031	0.0950	0.182	70	0.027
14	0.0641	0.0800	0.0800	0.033	0.0830	0.180	71	0.026
15	0.0571	0.0720	0.0720	0.035	0.0720	0.178	72	0.024
16	0.0508	0.0625	0.0640	0.037	0.0650	0.175	73	0.023
17	0.0453	0.0540	0.0560	0.039	0.0580	0.172	74	0.022
18	0.0403	0.0475	0.0480	0.041	0.0490	0.168	75	0.020
19	0.0359	0.0410	0.0400	0.043	0.0420	0.164	76	0.018
20	0.0320	0.0348	0.0360	0.045	0.0350	0.161	77	0.016
21	0.0285	0.0317	0.0320	0.047	0.0320	0.157	78	0.015
22	0.0253	0.0286	0.0280	0.049	0.0280	0.155	79	0.014
23	0.0226	0.0258	0.0240	0.051	0.0250	0.153	80	0.013
24	0.0201	0.0230	0.0220	0.055	0.0220	0.151	. . .	. . .
25	0.0179	0.0204	0.0200	0.059	0.0200	0.148	. . .	. . .
26	0.0159	0.0181	0.0180	0.063	0.0180	0.146	. . .	. . .
27	0.0142	0.0173	0.0164	0.067	0.0160	0.143	. . .	. . .
28	0.0126	0.0162	0.0148	0.071	0.0140	0.139	. . .	. . .
29	0.0113	0.0150	0.0136	0.075	0.0130	0.134	. . .	. . .
30	0.0100	0.0140	0.0124	0.080	0.0120	0.127	. . .	. . .
31	0.00893	0.0132	0.0116	0.085	0.0100	0.120	. . .	. . .
32	0.00795	0.0128	0.0108	0.090	0.0090	0.115	. . .	. . .
33	0.00708	0.0118	0.0100	0.095	0.0080	0.112	. . .	. .
34	0.00630	0.0104	0.0092	0.100	0.0070	0.110	. . .	. . .
35	0.00561	0.0095	0.0084	0.106	0.0050	0.108	. . .	. . .
36	0.00500	0.0090	0.0076	0.112	0.0040	0.106	. . .	. . .
37	0.00445	0.0085	0.0068	0.118	. . .	0.103	. . .	. . .
38	0.00396	0.0080	0.0060	0.124	. . .	0.101	. . .	. . .
39	0.00353	0.0075	0.0052	0.130	. . .	0.099	. . .	. . .
40	0.00314	0.0070	0.0048	0.138	. . .	0.097	. . .	. . .
41	0.00280	0.0066	0.0044	0.146	. . .	0.095	. . .	. . .
42	0.00249	0.0062	0.0040	0.154	. . .	0.092	. . .	. . .
43	0.00222	0.0060	0.0036	0.162	. . .	0.088	. . .	. . .
44	0.00198	0.0058	0.0032	0.170	. . .	0.085	. . .	. . .
45	0.00176	0.0055	0.0028	0.180	. . .	0.081	. . .	. . .
46	0.00157	0.0052	0.0024	. . .	. . .	0.079	. . .	. . .
47	0.00140	0.0050	0.0020	. . .	. . .	0.077	. . .	. . .
48	0.00124	0.0048	0.0016	. . .	. . .	0.075	. . .	. . .
49	0.00111	0.0046	0.0012	. . .	. . .	0.072	. . .	. . .
50	0.00099	0.0044	0.0010	. . .	. . .	0.069	. . .	. . .

*Also known as Washburn and Moen, American Steel and Wire Co., and Roebling wire gauges.

Table 2-3B
SHEET METAL GAUGES IN
APPROXIMATE
DECIMALS OF AN INCH

No. of sheet-metal gauge	Manufacturers' standard gauge for steel	Birmingham gauge (B.G.), for sheets, hoops	Gal-vanized sheet gauge	Zinc gauge
15/0	. . .	1.000	. . .	. . .
14/0	. . .	0.9583	. . .	. . .
13/0	. . .	0.9167	. . .	. . .
12/0	. . .	0.8750	. . .	. . .
11/0	. . .	0.8333	. . .	. . .
10/0	. . .	0.7917	. . .	. . .
9/0	. . .	0.7500	. . .	. . .
8/0	. . .	0.7083	. . .	. . .
7/0	. . .	0.6666	. . .	. . .
6/0	. . .	0.6250	. . .	. . .
5/0	. . .	0.5883	. . .	. . .
4/0	. . .	0.5416	. . .	. . .
3/0	. . .	0.5000	. . .	. . .
2/0	. . .	0.4452	. . .	. . .
1/0	. . .	0.3964	. . .	. . .
1	. . .	0.3532	. . .	. . .
2	. . .	0.3147	. . .	. . .
3	0.2391	0.2804	. . .	0.006
4	0.2242	0.2500	. . .	0.008
5	0.2092	0.2225	. . .	0.010
6	0.1943	0.1981	. . .	0.012
7	0.1793	0.1764	. . .	0.014
8	0.1644	0.1570	0.1681	0.016
9	0.1495	0.1398	0.1532	0.018
10	0.1345	0.1250	0.1382	0.020
11	0.1196	0.1113	0.1233	0.024
12	0.1046	0.0991	0.1084	0.028
13	0.0897	0.0882	0.0934	0.032
14	0.0747	0.0785	0.0785	0.036
15	0.0673	0.0699	0.0710	0.040
16	0.0598	0.0625	0.0635	0.045
17	0.0538	0.0556	0.0575	0.050
18	0.0478	0.0495	0.0516	0.055
19	0.0418	0.0440	0.0456	0.060
20	0.0359	0.0392	0.0396	0.070
21	0.0329	0.0349	0.0366	0.080
22	0.0299	0.03125	0.0336	0.090
23	0.0269	0.02782	0.0306	0.100
24	0.0239	0.02476	0.0276	0.125
25	0.0209	0.02204	0.0247	. . .
26	0.0179	0.01961	0.0217	. . .
27	0.0164	0.01745	0.0202	. . .
28	0.0149	0.01562	0.0187	. . .
29	0.0135	0.01390	0.0172	. . .
30	0.0120	0.01230	0.0157	. . .

Table 2-3B (Continued)

No. of sheet-metal gauge	Manufacturers' standard gauge for steel	Birmingham gauge (B.G.), for sheets, hoops	Gal-vanized sheet gauge	Zinc gauge
31	0.0105	0.01100	0.0142	. . .
32	0.0097	0.00980	0.0134	. . .
33	0.0090	0.00870	. . .	. . .
34	0.0082	0.00770	. . .	. . .
35	0.0075	0.00690	. . .	. . .
36	0.0067	0.00610	. . .	. . .
37	0.0064	0.00540	. . .	. . .
38	0.0060	0.00480	. . .	. . .
39	. . .	0.00430	. . .	. . .
40	. . .	0.00386	. . .	. . .
41	. . .	0.00343	. . .	. . .
42	. . .	0.00306	. . .	. . .
43	. . .	0.00272	. . .	. . .
44	. . .	0.00242	. . .	. . .
45	. . .	0.00215	. . .	. . .
46	. . .	0.00192	. . .	. . .
47	. . .	0.00170	. . .	. . .
48	. . .	0.00152	. . .	. . .
49	. . .	0.00135	. . .	. . .
50	. . .	0.00120	. . .	. . .
51	. . .	0.00107	. . .	. . .
52	. . .	0.00095	. . .	. . .
. . .	. . .	. . .	. . .	. . .

gauge of a wire one can either size it to one of the presized and numbered holes in a gauge plate or measure the diameter, in decimal value, and select that number value to which it corresponds in the chart. Sheet gauge sizes are determined by the same method. The decimal value is located within Table 2-3 and its gauge is then determined.

[2-9]
aluminum and aluminum alloys

Aluminum in its pure state is not generally used. Small amounts of other metals such as copper, silicon, magnesium, zinc, and nickel are added to increase the aluminum's strength or machinability. The various alloyed aluminums are then made into products with specific characteristics.

Aluminum alloys are produced in two classes:

1 / Non-heat treatable: Hardness is imparted by strain hardening.

2 / Heat treatable: Hardness is imparted by use of heat and special aging techniques.

Out of these two classes come a variety of alloys that are identified by a code consisting of a four-digit number followed by a letter and number which further describe the processes used in producing the alloyed product. To understand the code, let us look at the material specified by the code 2024—T351. In the first four-digit number (2024), each digit is used to specify the makeup of the material. The first digit identifies the type of alloy. The second digit identifies the alloy modification. The third and fourth digits identify the aluminum purity or the specific aluminum alloy.

The following list identifies the alloy defined by the first digit:

–1XXX   aluminum

–2XXX   copper

–3XXX   manganese

–4XXX   silicon

–5XXX   magnesium

–6XXX   magnesium and silicon

–7XXX   zinc

–8XXX   other element

–9XXX   for unused series

[NOTE]

The letter ''X'' precedes these four digits if the material is experimental in nature.

The second half of the coded number (T351) describes the condition of the material (hard, soft) and the method used in treating it. A temper range designated by the leters O, F, H, or T precedes the last group of numbers. Temper refers to the material's ability to spring back to its original state after loading. Annealed material has little or no spring and is very often used in products that must be bent or formed into a shape.

–F   as fabricated at the mill

–O   annealed (soft)

–H   strain hardened

–T   solution heat treated and aged

The digit immediately after the letter denotes the amount of temper. This number is from one to nine, indicating a low to high temper. The temper number 1 is the lowest temper, close to the annealed state of 0 temper, while the number 9 is the most highly tempered material. The second digit states that the material has had stress relieving treatment performed. The third digit indicates the method of stress relief used. This number is 1 for *stretching,* and 2 for *compression*; 3 through 9 are reserved for future development.

Aluminum has a variety of traits that make it a widely used material. The weight of aluminum is generally one-third that of other common metals. It has a natural resistance to the corrosive action of the atmosphere and many other chemical compounds. Because of its high thermal and electrical conductivity, it is being used in some applications for transmission of electrical power.

Aluminum fabricates easily and can be welded by all commercial methods, particularly the TIG welding arc process (tungsten–inert gas). Generally, in welding, the temper of the metal at the joint drops approximately by one-half to one temper grade. This drop is attributed to the heat of the weld's having an annealing effect on the metal at the joint. (To anneal a material is to heat the material to remove or prevent internal stress.)

Since the range of aluminum alloys is extremely diverse, Table 2-4 is presented to aid in the selection of the proper alloy for a specific job.

Aluminum products are available from suppliers in sheet, plate wire, rod, bar, tubing, pipe, and structural shapes, which include angle, I beams, and special extrusions for ornamental work.

Sheet products are generally considered to range up to a thickness of 0.190 inch. The most commonly produced gauge sheet thicknesses are numbers 24, 22, 20, 18, 16, 12, 11, and 10. Included within the sheet thickness range are fractional sizes such as 0.125 (⅛ inch) and 0.190, which is approximately a ³⁄₁₆-inch thickness.

Sheet aluminum is available in widths of 1, 2, 3, 4, 6, and 8 feet; lengths are from large coils running several hundred feet in length to standard lengths of 4, 8, 12, or 20 feet. It should be pointed out that almost all suppliers of metal products will cut or shear materials to your specified dimensions for a slight additional cost. This is important if many pieces are needed or if your facilities cannot handle your sizing needs economically. Remember, shearing pieces to size is always far more economical in both time and cost than saw cutting.

Plate thicknesses of aluminum are measured either in decimals of

Table 2-4
ALUMINUM ALLOY
APPLICATIONS

ALLOY SERIES	APPLICATIONS
11XX	Excellent forming properties for use in duct work, storage tanks, and cooking utensils.
20XX	Both high strength and good machining traits make it desirable for use in machine products for the aircraft and commercial products industries.
30XX 31XX	For forming all types of sheet metal products.
50XX	For decorative parts, general-purpose tubing and medium-strength welded structures.
60XX	High-strength type used in making flanges, bus bodies, ladders, and marine equipment.
70XX	Very high strength and hardness. This series is used extensively in the aircraft industry.

NOTE: Good or free machining material is defined as being easily cut or worked by the standard tools in the industry. Production of clean cutting chips, good surface finish and use of minimal cutting speed and feeding power are some of the main characteristics of free machining material.

an inch or fractional parts of an inch starting at $\frac{1}{4}$ inch and, depending on the supplier, ranging up to 4 inches. Thickness increments by $\frac{1}{16}$ inch cover the range from $\frac{1}{4}$ to $\frac{7}{8}$ inch; $\frac{1}{8}$-inch increments from $\frac{7}{8}$ to 1 inch; $\frac{1}{4}$-inch increments up to 2 inches and $\frac{1}{2}$-inch increments from 2 inches up. Thicker plate sections are normally not stocked and must be specially ordered from the mill. Plate widths most often start at 12 inches for the thinner plates and proceed to 24, 36, 48, and 60 inches for the thicker range of plates. Standard lengths for plates include a range that starts at 6, 8, and 12 feet.

Round rod is produced in a large range of aluminum alloys. Commercially, the diameters start at $\frac{1}{8}$ inch (0.125 inch) and run up to 8-inch diameters. Here again, larger diameters are available and must be specially ordered from the mill. Standard lengths may vary, but generally 12- and 20-foot lengths are produced.

For procurement of shapes such as square bar, hex bar, rectangular bar, tubing, and angle, the supplier should be consulted as to your needs. The range of shapes and sizes is so diverse that they are not discussed in this book.

[2-10]
copper, brass, and bronze

This section first describes copper, a metallic natural element, and then some of the more common copper alloys, brass and bronze.

copper

Copper, a natural element, is a relatively soft ductile metal that is light reddish brown in color. It has both high electrical and thermal conductive properties, which are used in electrical and heating applications.

Copper is highly corrosion resistant to atmosphere and water. When corrosion does take place on copper, a greenish blue film of copper sulphate is formed. This film of copper sulphate is somewhat water soluble and can generally be removed by brushing with soapy water.

To anneal copper products, the following procedure is recommended. Heat the piece to a temperature of 900° to 1000°F and immediately water quench it. *Quenching is a process whereby a heated material is suddenly cooled by plunging it into a liquid, usually water or oil, to harden or anneal it.*

brass

Brass is a general term applied to an alloy that has copper as its base metal. Zinc is alloyed with the copper in varying degrees to produce a range of brasses which include: *red brass, low brass, cartridge brass, yellow brass,* and *muntz metal,* which has the highest zinc content (approximately 40 percent). These brass alloys have a hardness range from soft (red brass) to hard (yellow brass and muntz metal).

leaded brass

To improve good cutting and machining action, a group of leaded brass alloys is made. The introduction of small amounts of lead enhances the cutting and finishing characteristics of this type of brass. Leaded brass includes leaded commercial bronze, leaded brass tubing, and free cutting brass, sometimes denoted as free machining (FM). Leaded brass products are highly recommended where extensive machining is to be performed.

bronze

By the addition of traceable amounts of tin into the basic brass alloy, a material called bronze is produced. Bronze is very hard and has excellent qualities when used as sleeve bearings in small- to medium-sized machines. The name *Tobin bronze* is assigned to this particular type of bronze.

phosphor bronze

The addition of phosphor into most alloys imparts a tough but somewhat brittle effect to the end product. When added to the basic bronze alloy in small amounts, a product known as phosphor bronze is produced.

Phosphor bronze alloys have high strength, good corrosion resistance, and excellent bearing and spring properties. These spring properties are used in the manufacture of coil and spring leaf pieces. When needed, a free machining form of this alloy is available and should be specified when ordered, normally by the letters (FM).

When one is ordering either the phosphor bronze wire or sheet, several grades of temper are available. Generally, a specification as to hardness ranges from half hard to full hard, which has the greatest spring temper characteristics. If the need for a soft condition arises, a fully annealed material should be specified.

eighteen percent
nickel-silver alloy

An 18 percent nickel-silver alloy of copper is available for use in forming small parts in draw and forming dies. This alloy has strong physical properties, good corrosion resistance, and is silvery white in color. Due to its particular alloy, the material is very malleable and ductile, making it an excellent choice for many forming operations.

The addition of both silver and nickel to the base metal of copper makes the cost of the material higher than the more common brass.

[2-11]
welding, brazing, and soldering copper and copper alloys

Both copper and its range of brass products can be brazed with a silver or brass rod and a gas torch. When a torch is used, the material, particularly the hardened brasses, tends to anneal slightly.

Soldering with the low-temperature tin/lead or silver solders is quite easily performed with both copper and brass products. Cleaning of the material with fine steel wool is recommended prior to all soldering operations. Soldering fluids, which further clean and prepare the metal surface, are suggested for ease of completing a soldering joint.

Electric inert gas welding (TIG) can be performed on small assemblies of copper only. Brass cannot be welded, because its alloys burn out, causing destruction of the metal and metal fume poisoning. Large copper pieces are difficult to TIG weld, since large amounts of heat are required to reach the weld heat temperature.

machining properties of copper and copper alloys

Copper is very difficult to machine because of its soft gummy texture. Very often, the material being removed sticks and bonds on the cutting tool. This bonding can be reduced by using kerosene during cutting.

Brass and bronzes have machining properties that run from fair to excellent. The red brass form is slightly better than copper to machine, and the leaded brasses have very good machining properties. Use of somewhat dull or rounded cutting edges is recommended to prevent digging or chipping of the brass by the particular cutting tool.

[2-12]
steels (common)

Steel is a by-product of cast iron and other additives that have been specially alloyed by an open hearth furnace, a basic oxygen furnace (BOF), or an electric furnace process. By the deletion or addition of a variety of materials during the molten state, a range of steels can be produced from the common low carbon steel to the high-strength, corrosion-resistant stainless steels.

To identify the very diverse range of steels, a numbering system is used. The basic system in common use is the SAE method of notation (Society of Automotive Engineers). This system of notation consists of a four- or five-digit number. As certain alloys become very complex in structure, the addition of a letter or a chemical element symbol may be added.

The American Iron and Steel Institute (AISI) also has its own notation system for steel alloys. The usual notation is termed *AISI type*. The two numbering systems, in almost all cases, are identical except in the stainless groups. The AISI number for this group merely uses the last three digits of the SAE number for the type of stainless. For example, a particular grade of chromium stainless steel is noted in the SAE notation as 51403. The AISI notation merely uses the last three digits and therefore denotes this grade of steel as AISI type 403. Some manufacturers use either or both notations in their materials catalog. Later in this section, tables denoting both notation systems are presented along with some of their applications.

The SAE numbering system is by far the most used system in both ordering or specifying a particular type of steel. The first digit of the notation indicates the class or type of steel that the product is made from; the second digit is used for alloy steels and gives the approximate percentage of the main alloy. Table 2-5 defines the first two digits of the notation. The last two or three digits in the SAE system of notation denote the average carbon content of the steel in "points," or hundredths of one percent.

To summarize the meaning of the SAE number or grade of steel, let us look at an SAE 1020 steel. The digit 1 means that it is a carbon steel. The 0 following it means that it is not an alloy-type steel. The last two digits, 20, mean that it has 20 points of carbon or 0.2 percent carbon in its makeup.

characteristics of carbon steels

The SAE steels 1006, 1008, 1010, and 1015 are the lowest-carbon-content steels available. These grades are selected in applications where the product is to be formed by drawing through dies to produce rod wire or press formed shapes using dies. Its main uses are in producing such items as automotive body parts, soft wire, and rivets for cold or hammer forming. These grades of steel are not to be used where strength is the prime consideration.

Machining of the 1006, 1008, 1010, and 1015 group is not performed

Table 2-5
SAE NOTATION SYSTEM
FOR STEEL ALLOYS
(first two digits)

1.	Carbon steel	10XX
	(free machining type)	11XX
2.	Manganese steel	13XX
3.	Nickel steels	23XX and 24XX
4.	Nickel chrome steels	31XX
		33XX
		303XX
5.	Molybdenum steels	40XX
6.	Chrome/molybdenum steel	41XX
7.	Nickel/chrome/molybdenum steel	43XX
		47XX
		86XX
		87XX
		93XX
		98XX
8.	Nickel/molybdenum steel	46XX
		48XX
9.	Chrome steels	50XX
		51XX
		501XX
		511XX
		521XX
	Corrosion and heat resistant	514XX/515XX
10.	Chrome/vanadium steel	61XX
11.	Silicon/manganese steel	92XX

well and is not recommended for production of machine parts. However, steels in this group are both easily and effectively welded by either electric arc or gas welding methods.

SAE 1016, 1017, 1018, 1019, 1020, 1021, 1022, 1023, 1024, 1025, 1026, 1027, 1030 (1016 to 1030 range) steels

This group of steels has improved carbon content, which increases their strength and also reduces their ductility. Bolts and tubing are made from steels in the 1020 to 1021 range. Machining of parts within this group is still not of the free machining grade. This range of steels is used in forming workpieces by use of cold or heat processes.

For heat treating or hardening of thin sections of steels, the SAE grades of 1016 to 1019 are used. Heavy work sections generally use SAE 1022 and 1024. Where greater hardness is required, the SAE 1025 and 1030 grades of steels are used. When any steel is heat treated, accurate control of both heating and quenching must be exercised.

SAE 1020 bar stock is used in some screw machine products. This material can be welded and brazed using the common commercial methods.

SAE 1030 to 1052 range

This group of steels is generally considered to be the medium carbon-type steels. A steel from this group is selected when the application requires higher strength and there is a need to harden by heat treating or cold working. Because of its strength, this SAE range of steel is used to produce many products in the automotive industry.

Machining can be performed by conventional methods, but as its carbon content increases cutting edge contact to metal, wear results in frequent dulling with subsequent tool resharpening required. All steels in this range can be used for forging processes and can be heat treated to specific requirements.

SAE 1030 to 1052 steels can be welded. Welding at the higher carbon levels should be performed with some caution. Rapid cooling of welded joints can cause cracks to develop which destroy the strength of the joint.

SAE 1055 to 1095 range

Steels in the 1055 to 1095 range are high-carbon steels. Due to an excess of carbon, cold forming of these grades is not recommended. The main applications of this range are in the manufacture of spring-type products, which include springs, music wire, rake teeth, plowshares, and scraper blades—or any application where spring temper and abrasive resistance are required.

Machining of steels in the 1055 to 1095 range is quite difficult and must be approached with the tougher alloyed cutting tools. These grades can be fully hardened and tempered by the standard practices. Welding is difficult and is not recommended.

SAE 1111 to 1151 range

To answer the needs of free machining products, the 1100 series steels are made. The free machining quality of these steels is achieved through the addition of sulphur to the alloy. The addition of sulphur, however, reduces the cold forming, welding, and forging properties of the product. In the production of commercial fasteners, where strength is not the main factor, this steel is used extensively.

Heat treatment is possible in the range of SAE 1115 through 1151. Naturally, the higher-carbon steels allow for deeper penetration in the hardening process. If the end product is to be welded, the use of this grade of steel is not recommended.

[2-13]
stainless steels

With the addition of elements such as chromium, nickel, vanadium, and molybdenum to the basic steel composition, a grade of steel known as *stainless* is produced. This product exhibits excellent strength and corrosion resistance. Because of the wide use of this type of steel, the cost has dropped; hence, it is being used where other types of common steel were previously used.

When machining operations are performed on many grades of stainless steels, the cutting-edge-to-metal contact will sometimes cause work hardening of the metal. This problem develops usually when a cutting tool is allowed to rub or burnish the metal in contact without proper cutting pressure. When this situation is encountered, all lubrication should be removed from the work area. The tool should then be resharpened and again brought in contact with the metal surface. A slow rotation coupled with a heavy feed should be used. Once the tool has broken through this hardened shell, normal lubrication can be applied and the cutting operation continued.

When stainless steel is discussed, three terms are used to describe its workability and structure: *austenitic, martensitic,* and *ferritic.* Austenitic stainless steel refers to the fact that, when annealed, the structure is composed of a micrograin structure of austenite. This grade of steel cannot be work hardened and is nonmagnetic unless severely cold worked.

Martensitic stainless steel is so named because when hardened, its structure is composed of a micrograin structure of martensite. This type of steel is magnetic and, owing to a high carbon content, can be hardened.

Ferritic grades of stainless steels get their name from the micrograin structure of alpha ferrite when in the annealed state. This grade is magnetic, and does not harden well. Table 2-6 shows the AISI grades and their ranges.

Table 2-6
STAINLESS STEELS—AISI TYPE AND GRADES

GRADES	AISI TYPE
Austenitic	301 to 347
Martensitic	403, 410, 414, 416, 420, 431, 440
Ferritic	430, 442, 446

Table 2-7 is provided to aid the technician in selecting austenitic stainless steels to meet specific job requirements. Table 2-8 is provided to aid the technician in selecting martensitic steels. Ferritic types of stainless steel exhibit characteristics and workability similar to the martensitic types within the AISI range and thus are not tabled.

Table 2-7
AUSTENITIC STEELS
(not capable of heat treating)

AISI TYPE	APPLICATIONS
301, 302	Food trays, equipment, spun forms, or most sheet formed sections
303	Free machining type—used to produce all forms of machine products, such as screws, shafts, rolls
304	Free machining type—same as type 303, but has excellent welding abilities (*NOTE:* 304L type same as 304, but can be polished without surface blemishes)
309	Free machining, weldable, free forming, used in heated environments such as kiln linings, furnace parts, oil and gas combustion chambers
316	Hard machining, excellent corrosion resistance. Used in textile, paper, and chemical industries
321 to 347	Hard machining, poor welding, same applications as 316 type

Table 2-8
MARTENSITIC STEELS
(capable of heat treating)

AISI TYPE	APPLICATIONS
410	Used for cold headed products such as screws, bolts, cutlery, conveyor parts, furnace and stove parts where temperature does not exceed 1250° F.
416	Free machining type; used in all types of production machine tools, particularly in screw manufacturing.
420	Used in the manufacture of dental and surgical instruments; harder machining than type 416; welding is poor.
430	Because of strength and resistance to heat, it is used in oil burners, heat exchangers, combustion chambers and annealing furnaces. Due to hardening of welded joints, it is not recommended for shock- or vibration-type applications.
440	These alloys are used where the highest strength and corrosion resistance are needed. Used in valves, high-grade cutlery, and where abrasion resistant parts are required. Welding is not recommended.
446	Good heat and abrasion resistance. Used for furnace floor plates and oil burner combustion chambers. Welding is poor to fair.

[2-14]
summary

The single purpose of both Chapters 1 and 2 was that of introducing the reader to the basic definitions, terms, types, and forms of the metal products in general use.

It is hoped that what has been presented in these two chapters will give you the confidence and understanding needed when you encounter the materials of this artistic and highly skilled trade.

review questions

2-1 / In the formation of a finished metal product such as a bar or a rod, what three processes can be used?

2-2 / If a metal product of both good surface finish and physical dimensions were required, what choices would you have?

2-3 / What is the cause of the grainy surface that is found on hot rolled metal products?

2-4 / Why do cold rolled products have better surface and size features than hot rolled products?

2-5 / One of the basic requirements in extruded products is that the metal be ductile. If the metal is not of a ductile nature, what can be done to increase its ductility?

2-6 / What is the difference between pipe and tubing? Consider ½ inch pipe and ½ inch tubing.

2-7 / The American Wire or Brown & Sharpe gauge system is used exclusively for what types of wire?

2-8 / A drawing produced in England specifies 4 lengths of copper wire 0.0180 dia. (imperial wire gauge). Select the American gauge number that most closely matches this size.

2-9 / In measuring several sheets of steel used in the fabrication of a workpiece, the following thicknesses were noted:
Sheet 1 = 0.015 inches thick
Sheet 2 = 0.061 inches thick
Sheet 3 = 0.031 inches thick
Specify the above thicknesses in their sheet gauge numbers.

2-10 / What are the weight per cubic foot and the melting temperature of aluminum?

2-11 / Name the two methods used in hardening aluminum alloys.

2-12 / Consider the aluminum alloy 6061-T6. What is its main alloy? Is this an annealed, tempered, or hardened product? Does it have poor, fair, or high strength?

2-13 / Copper, a basic metal, is used to form what two common alloyed by-products?

2-14 / Define *quenching* as related to metals.

2-15 / Two systems are used to identify steel products. What are they, and how are they different?

2-16 / Describe the meaning of *SAE 1082.*

2-17 / Select an SAE grade of carbon steel that would best produce each of the following metal parts: bailing wire, tubing, rivets, ice scraper blades, springs (leaf or coil), metal formings where hardness is not essential.

2-18 / What are the main characteristics of stainless steels?

2-19 / What AISI type of stainless steel is most commonly used in sheet metal formed sections?

2-20 / What AISI type of stainless steel is used often in dental instruments?

2-21 / AISI type 316 is used often in food processing equipment. Why do you think this type was chosen?

3

basic hand tools

[3-1]
introduction

With our introduction to the various metal products, along with their specific characteristics given in the previous chapters, we shall begin with the basic hand tools used by the technician in working with the product itself.

Hand tools are those tools whose single purpose is to: measure, gauge, aid in the layout of a workpiece, strike, punch, scribe, drill, clamp, shear, torque, and shave.

[3-2]
measuring tools

A prerequisite in any trade where an accurate layout is to be made from
a print or sketch is a set of measuring standards or measuring tools. These
measuring tools are used to produce a workpiece to accurate dimensions
of length, width, thickness, and angular requirements.

steel tapes

A basic measuring tool of almost daily use is the flexible pocket steel tape.
These measuring tapes are used for measuring linear (straight line)
distances and curved surfaces such as the circumference of a cylinder.

Steel tapes are available in several lengths ranging from 72 inches
(6 feet), 96 inches (8 feet), 120 inches (10 feet), up to a 1200-inch (100-
foot) tape. The steel tape, with its graduations, is produced in widths of
$\frac{3}{8}$-inch, $\frac{1}{2}$-inch, and $\frac{5}{8}$-inch spring tempered steel. The spring temper in
the tape affords both strength and durability and allows it to be stored
within its case. The tape is coiled within the case and can be withdrawn
by hand for use. After use, either hand pushing into the case or pressing
a rewind button conveniently stores the measuring tape. A vertical metal
tab at the 0-inch end of the tape is used to hold the tape at an edge
during a measurement.

Graduations along the tape are in most cases, by $\frac{1}{16}$-inch increments. The tape is marked at inch increments generally with a large
marker line with its inch position value indicated. Between each inch
increment $\frac{1}{4}$-inch, $\frac{1}{8}$-inch, and $\frac{1}{16}$-inch increments appear. Thus, measurements with the above tape can be made within an accuracy of $\frac{1}{16}$ of
an inch. In the longer tapes, the measuring scale is indicated in foot
increments, inch increments, and $\frac{1}{8}$-inch increments. These larger tapes
have general use in the building and surveying fields.

Since this is a measuring tool, care should be exercised in maintaining its usefulness. Because the tape is made of spring temper steel, it
should never be bent at any sharp corners or edges. Severe bends will
produce cracks and in some cases fracture the tape completely apart.
Should grease, dirt, or other foreign materials cling to the tape during a
measurement, a dry soft cotton cloth or paper tissue should be used to
clean its surface prior to storage. Moisture within the case can cause
rusting if allowed to set. If moisture is suspected, wipe the fully extended

blade with a dry cloth. Allow the casing to rest near a light bulb; the heat will dry out the remaining moisture. Above all, never wipe the graduated tape with any solvent, particularly alcohol or acetone, as this could dissolve the baked enamel graduations on the tape.

steel scales

When it is required to measure linear distances to more accurate dimensions than a steel tape can provide, the steel scale is used. Steel scales are produced in either a semi-flexible or a rigid state, the material being either steel or stainless steel. Commercial lengths include 6-inch, 12-inch, 18-inch, 24-inch, 36-inch, and 48-inch scales.

Unlike the steel tape, whose general measuring accuracy is $\frac{1}{16}$ inch, the steel scale can measure to an accuracy of $\frac{1}{64}$ inch. This is possible because the increments are ruled or engraved into the metal and can thus be spaced more closely than those printed on tape measures.

The scale graduations of steel scales can be procured in various graduations in both the metric and English system of measure. The scale of most interest to the technician is that which has graduations noted in inch, $\frac{1}{4}$-inch, $\frac{1}{8}$-inch, $\frac{1}{16}$-inch, $\frac{1}{32}$-inch, and $\frac{1}{64}$-inch increments. These increments are located along the length of each of the scale's four edges. Typically, each of the scales is incremented and so noted at the *"even inch positions."* The general grouping of the graduations along each of the four long edges of the scale is

EDGE NO.	DIVISIONS INDICATED
1	$\frac{1}{4}$ and $\frac{1}{8}$ inch
2	$\frac{1}{4}$ and $\frac{1}{16}$ inch
3	$\frac{1}{8}$ and $\frac{1}{32}$ inch
4	$\frac{1}{8}$ and $\frac{1}{64}$ inch

As an aid, several manufacturers have added, at the $\frac{1}{8}$-inch increments on both the $\frac{1}{32}$- and $\frac{1}{64}$-inch edges, the numerical value of the increment at each position. For example, in looking at the $\frac{1}{32}$-inch increment edge and reading from left to right, you will see small engraved number values at each $\frac{1}{8}$-inch increment. Typically, on the $\frac{1}{32}$-inch edge increments would read 4, 8, 12, 16, 20, 24, 28. For example, if a measurement falls between 16 and 20, one merely counts the increments to the point or line being measured and adds them to 16. Thus, the reading would be 16 ($\frac{1}{32}$-inch parts) plus the additional $\frac{1}{32}$-inch parts to the line or point in measure. You can readily see that this method is faster than if you had to count the number of increments one by one from the end of the scale. On the $\frac{1}{64}$-inch increment edge, the following engraved numbers would appear at the $\frac{1}{8}$-inch increments: 8, 16, 24, 32, 40, 48, and 56.

When you purchase a scale, it is recommended that you buy one of good quality and, if possible, in stainless steel or the satin chrome-plated grade. Both of the above are resistant to tarnish or rust. The satin chrome grade is by far the clearest to read, as its finish will not allow lighting to reflect into your eyes during a measurement. A 6-inch and an 18-inch scale are a good basic choice.

Steel scales should be protected from dirt and abrasive particles by wiping with a soft cotton cloth. They should be stored, when not in use, in either a protective wooden box or plastic carrying case. Rubbing contact with other tools should be avoided as this can cause rub marks which in turn affect the engraved scale, and ultimately its accuracy.

combination set

Possibly the most important tool to the sheet metal technician is the square head, bevel protractor and scale, often called a *combination set*. This tool, with the square head and bevel protractor, allows a technician to produce perpendicular (vertical) lines, to step off the positions of holes or centers of circles, and to produce or measure accurately lines or angles.

The square head is an accurately machined casting that contains three specific surfaces of reference: a long base surface, a surface at an angle of 90 degrees to the base and a surface at an angle of 45 degrees to the base.

A groove, machined perpendicular to the long base, allows for a grooved steel scale to be inserted. This scale, when secured with the locking screw within the head, forms a 90-degree angle with the base edge.

This adjustable feature also allows specific dimensions to be set with respect to the base and locked; thus, the locations of points or lines can be located on flat work surfaces.

A second feature of the square head and scale is its use in *squaring* a piece of stock. Squaring merely means that one either checks or produces a vertical side or edge to an existing edge.

The bevel protractor is a highly accurate device for producing or measuring angles within one-twelfth of a specified degree or 5 minutes (5′). This tool has a base or reference edge like that of the square head. Located within the casting is a dial indicating one-degree increments over a range of 0 to 180 degrees. The scale, reading in a counterclockwise direction, is denoted as 0 to 90 degrees, while the second half reads 90 to 0 degrees. The dial contains a groove and clamp screw to hold a scale as described in the square head. This dial, with its scale clamp, is rotatable

Figure 3-1 — Combination set. *(Courtesy of L.S. Starrett Co.)*

within the main casting of the protractor. Rotation is achieved by loosening the two knurled locking screws within the casting.

Three fixed reference lines are denoted on the fixed frame, adjacent to the inner dial. These lines are exactly 90 degrees apart from each other and are noted by "O" marks. It is in relation to these marks that angles are read or produced.

To increase the accuracy of measurement, some protractors are equipped with a vernier scale (Fig. 3-2). The vernier scale consists of 12 division lines located on either side of its "O" point. Thus, an accuracy of degree measurement can be made within one-twelfth of a degree or 5 minutes.

Let us return to Fig. 3-2 and begin our discussion on reading the vernier correctly. First, let us determine the whole degree value as indicated by the alignment of the zero on the vernier and the last whole degree on the degree scale. As indicated, there are 50 whole degrees shown (as read from right to left).

The next step is to determine the incremental parts of a degree beyond our 50-degree reading. Since we have read our original angle from right to left, we must use the left side of the vernier. Begin looking for that line on the vernier that aligns with one of the whole degree lines on the rim. The line immediately after the 15-minute value of the vernier aligns with a whole degree value on the outer edge. Remember that each division has a value of 5 minutes, so our vernier reading would be 15 minutes + 5 minutes = 20 minutes. The actual value of our illustrated angle is, therefore, 50° 20'. Remember, the right side of the vernier is used when the whole degree value is read from left to right.

The above tools, if maintained, will give years of accurate service. Clean, oil, and store these tools in a manner whereby rust, dents, or nicks are not produced on the machined reference surfaces.

Figure 3-2 — Vernier scale. *(Courtesy of L.S. Starrett Co.)*

outside micrometer caliper

Up to this point, we have been able to measure with a tape measure accurately to ⅟₁₆ inch (0.0625 inch). The steel scale then allowed us to measure to an accuracy of ⅟₆₄ inch (0.0154 inch). We now shall discuss a measuring tool that will measure thicknesses or diameters to an accuracy of one one-thousandth of an inch (0.001 inch). This precision measuring tool is called the *outside micrometer caliper* (Fig. 3-3).

The outside micrometer caliper, often called a ''mike,'' is a tool that determines measurements in decimal notation only.

The English micrometer has three indicators of measurement, the major scale noted from 0 to 10 on the sleeve, where the decimal value between each major sleeve division is ⅟₁₀ inch or 0.100 inch. The second indicator is the minor sleeve divisions located between each major divi-

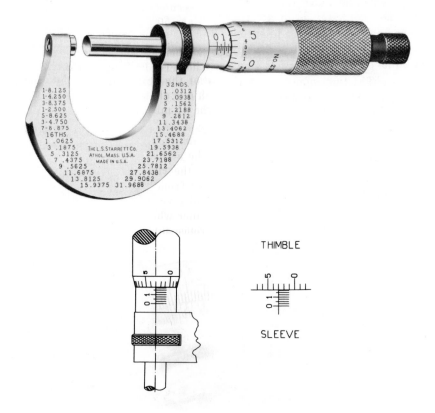

Figure 3-3 — Outside micrometer caliper. *(Courtesy of L.S. Starrett Co.)*

sion. There are four minor divisions between each; thus each division is one-fourth of 0.100 inch or 0.025 inch in value. The third and final measuring scale is the thimble scale. This scale has 25 divisions indicated. The value of each division on the thimble is 0.001 inch (one one-thousandth of an inch).

Determining the decimal size of a workpiece thus entails evaluating the three indicator values, or the value of the largest major scale value plus the sum of the whole increments of the minor sleeve divisions immediately after it plus the sum of the divisions indicated on the thimble.

To go through the exercise of using a "thousandths indicating mike," refer to Fig. 3-3.

The anvils of the micrometer are brought to the area of measurement. Using the ratchet knob at the end of the thimble, turn the thimble until the anvils are almost in contact with the workpiece. Turn the thimble more slowly until contact is made. Allow the ratchet to click several times. Remove the mike by sliding it off the workpiece. In the case of a round workpiece, move the anvils back and forth until the maximum diameter is reached.

To read a typical setting return to Fig. 3-3 and perform the following observations:

Major sleeve divisions	$1 \times 0.100 =$	0.100
Minor sleeve divisions	$3 \times 0.025 =$	0.075
Thimble divisions	$3 \times 0.001 =$	0.003
By addition		0.178

Until you develop the ability to read and interpret directly, you should perform the calculations demonstrated above for size measurement.

Micrometers are available in ranges of 0 to 1 inch, 1 to 2 inches, 2 to 3 inches, up to and including 5 to 6 inches. The sheet metal technician will find that almost all of his needs will be filled by the 0-to-1-inch micrometer.

Care should be exercised in both usage and storage. Keep the anvil tips clean at all times and remove dirt and abrasives with a soft cloth. A light coat of oil over the entire tool during storage is essential to keep it from tarnishing or rusting. Never store a micrometer with its anvils together, as heat can expand and spring the main frame. A check of accuracy can be performed as follows. Close the anvils of the micrometer until the ratchet is heard. The thimble reading should have the zero (0) line aligned with the longitudinal line, as shown in Fig. 3-3. Adjustment to zero should adhere to the manufacturer's recommended method.

sheet and wire gauges

A tool that proves to be of great aid to the sheet metal mechanic is a sheet and wire gauge. These tools are made of hardened steel with *sized* openings located about their circular edge (Fig. 3-4). A slot with its corresponding gauge size is noted, while on the opposite face of the gauge the decimal value of the gauge is given.

The wire gauge should be of the Brown & Sharpe or American Steel and Wire Co. (Washburn and Moen) standard. The gauge range of wire and sheet generally includes sizes 0 to 36.

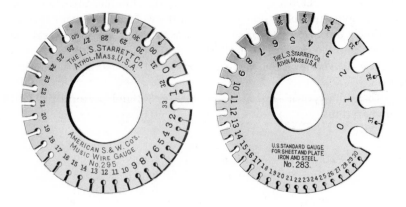

Figure 3-4 — Wire and sheet gauges. *(Courtesy of L.S. Starrett Co.)*

Remember that the Brown & Sharpe system is used for all metal products, except steel and iron. When steel or iron products are gauged, the American Steel and Wire Co. (Washburn and Moen) gauge is used.

Gauging with this tool involves a go–no go operation. A size determination is achieved by merely selecting two consecutive slots. One fits the workpiece, and one does not; hence a *go–no go* situation. The gauged slot that allows the workpiece to just enter is the gauge value of the material.

Care of these tools is minimal; a light coating of oil should be applied to their surfaces during periods of nonuse.

An an alternative to this tool, the 0-to-1-inch micrometer may be used to determine the decimal size of the material. Use of the wire and sheet gauge table will then give the gauge number.

[3-3]
scribing tools

To produce lines or circles on paper, the standard tools are simply a pencil and a compass with a pencil attached to one leg. In hard surface layout such as that on a metal sheet, marking tools are required that scratch or scribe the surface of the metal.

Figure 3-5 shows the two basic scribing tools for the metal trade, a scriber and a divider. The scriber is equipped with a hard-pointed metal tip. Its purpose is to scribe straight lines on hard surfaces with the aid of a steel scale or straight edge. To scribe shapes such as circles or arcs or to space off lengths along a scribed line, the divider is used. This tool is equipped with two legs that are adjustable over a given range called the *size* of the divider. Thus a 6-inch divider will allow adjustment between leg points from nearly 0 to 6 inches. If the divider is used as a compass,

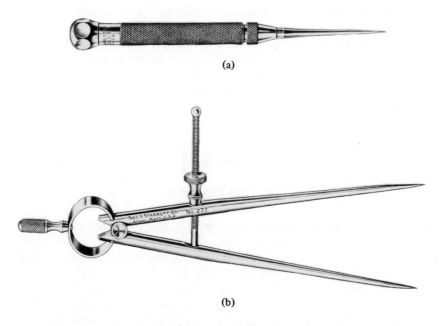

(a)

(b)

Figure 3-5 — (a) Scriber. (b) Divider. *(Courtesy of L.S. Starrett Co.)*

with one leg at the center, circles with diameters of approximately ½ inch through 12 inches can be scribed.

Two basic forms of dividers exist: the spring divider and the quick release divider. The spring divider is so called because a circular leaf spring is located at the pivot point of the two legs. This supplies a force to propel the two legs apart. Located between the spring and divider tips is a threaded shaft with an adjusting knob. This knob restrains and compresses the spring joint, thereby allowing for accurate adjustment of the point tips.

The quick release version has two features that make it the more favored tool of the two. A section of metal arc is permanently affixed to one of the legs. This arc then passes through a slot in the second leg with a locking screw so that it can be made to clamp and lock the two legs together.

A vernier adjust knob is used to finely open or close the tips to a required setting. The main feature of this form of divider is that one can more rapidly change and set tip dimensions than one can in the spring joint-screw adjust type.

Two sizes are recommended to meet general needs; they are 2-inch dividers and 6-inch dividers. The 2-inch divider is available only in the spring joint, whereas in the 6-inch or larger size, both spring and quick release types are available.

In both storage and use, protect the tip points from damage. When storing the spring joint type, allow the divider to be adjusted to its maximum opening with the points covered with pieces of cork or plastic. This will ensure long life to the spring. A fine coating of oil is essential, as it is for all metal tools of this nature.

[3-4]
hammers

Three types of hammers most often used in the sheet metal trades are ball peen, tinner's, and soft face (Fig. 3-6).

The ball peen, the most diverse of the hammers, is used to strike punches or chisels with its flat face, while the ball end is used in forming thin metal sections (called peening). Rivets can also be formed and peened with this type of hammer. These hammers are cataloged by the weights of their heads with a range of 2 to 20 ounces. The most practical weight is the 10-ounce size. The ball peen hammer should under no cir-

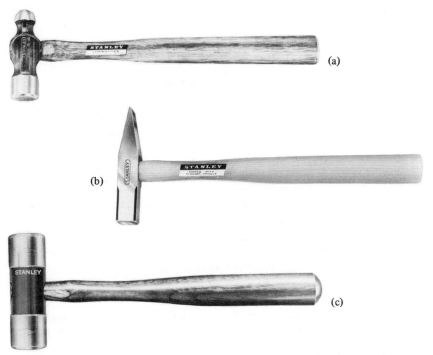

Figure 3-6 — Hammers. (a) Ball peen. (b) Tinner's riveting. (c) Soft face. *(Courtesy of The Stanley Works)*

cumstances be used to drive nails, as its face is not designed for this practice.

Tinners riveting hammers mainly answer the needs of the craftsman in free-forming sheet metal pieces. The flat face is used to form the heads on small rivets, while the tapered end opposite the flat head is used to form bends or seams in thin sheet metal sections, such as duct work, rain spouting, or copper flashing used on the roofs of buildings. Tinners hammers are, like the ball peen, listed as to head weight. The range generally runs from 8 to 20 ounces, with the 16-ounce weight being a good choice.

Soft face hammers are diverse in makeup, and are available in plastic, hard rubber or cowhide. These hammers are designed to work fine finished surfaces or delicate assembly parts without marring or denting.

The plastic or hard rubber face hammers are the most popular, since they can be obtained with replaceable faces should one or both become damaged. Weight ranges normally include 1½-ounce to 32-ounce weight. Either an 8- or a 16-ounce weight will suffice for most needs.

[3-5]
punches

Two forms of punches most often used in the metal trades are the prick punch and the center punch (Fig. 3-7).

The prick punch is most often used to mark the location of lines, line intersections, or centers of circles. Its long slender point of approximately 20 to 30 degrees is useful in that it produces conical holes in the workpiece, in which dividers or other pointed measuring tools may be referenced.

To produce more legible and larger marks on a workpiece after a layout, the center punch is used. The center punch has a tip angle of approximately 118 to 120 degrees. This punch thus produces a conical hole that approximates the tip angle of a drill bit; consequently, drills of small diameters may be used directly in a center-punched hole.

Both prick and center punches are made in various lengths, in the form of either a cylinder or a hexagon cross section. Lengths can be obtained in 4 to 6 inches. The 4-inch length is the most popular.

After the point has dulled, a punch is brought back to a useful condition by regrinding the conical tip as originally shaped. A good tip in grinding is to grind from the point of the cone back while rotating the punch against the grinding wheel. This produces a fine sharp point.

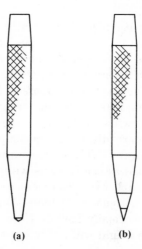

(a)   (b)

Figure 3-7 — Punches. (a) Center. (b) Prick.

[3-6]
chisels

A tool that is essential in the sheet metal technician's toolbox is the chisel. A basic set of cold chisels includes the flat, cape, round nose, and diamond point types (Fig. 3-8).

These tools are designed to shear, cut, or gouge metal through the striking action of a hammer at the face end. The working end of each of

(a)

(b)

(c)

(d)

Figure 3-8 — Basic chisel forms. (a) Flat. (b) Cape. (c) Diamond point. (d) Round nose. *(Courtesy of The Stanley Works)*

these chisels is heat treated for hardness, while the striking end is somewhat softer.

The *flat chisel* is designed to shear through metal sheet or small rods or to remove rusted bolt, nut, or rivet heads. This chisel is selected by the width of cut; commercial widths range from $\frac{3}{16}$ inch to 1 inch.

The *cape chisel* is designed to cut or shave grooves, keyways, or slots in metal. This chisel is selected by its width of cutting surface, which ranges from $\frac{1}{8}$ inch to $\frac{7}{8}$ inch.

The *round nose chisel* serves a specific need in that it produces grooves in metal that are semicircular in form. This requirement is most often encountered when oil grooves must be produced in a workpiece, although decorative designs are also created with this tool. The curved width of the chisel defines its size. The round nose chisel can be procured with a grooving range of from $\frac{1}{8}$ inch to $\frac{7}{8}$ inch.

The *diamond point* chisel serves specific requirements: to cut vee-shaped grooves, to sharpen or square corners in castings, and to turn out broken studs or rounded nuts. The working end of this chisel is triangular in cross section. It is specified by its size range of $\frac{1}{8}$ inch through $\frac{7}{8}$ inch.

The above chisels can be purchased either singly or in sets. Lengths normally range from 5 to 9 inches, with the 6-inch length being the popular. Care of these tools falls into two areas, maintaining a sharp cutting edge and the removal by grinding of the mushrooming metal at the strik-ing end. A coat of oil during storage will protect the tool from rust.

[3-7]
pliers

Pliers are tools designed to apply enhanced hand power to grip, bend, form, or cut hard materials or forms. A wide variety of pliers is made, but we shall discuss only those that have immediate need in the sheet metal trade.

The three basic plier forms that will be discussed are the combina-tion, or slip joint, the duck bill, and the side cutter, shown in Fig. 3-9. Locking pliers will be discussed in the following section.

The *combination plier,* also called the slip joint, is used to hold, bend, or twist small metal pieces of either a flat or round shape. The slip joint is incorporated quickly to adjust the gripping range of the jaws when required.

The flat sections of the jaws are used to grip flat material to either pull or bend. The large serrations are used to grasp round sections when turning or twisting is necessary.

The work opening to length size of the plier falls into two main sizes: a ¾-inch opening for a 5-inch length and a 1½-inch opening for a 10-inch length.

The *duck bill plier* is employed when it is necessary to make small bends in sheet metal. The jaws of this plier, while serrated for grip, are such that they will not mar the metal being bent. The width of jaw nor-mally ranges from ⅜ inch to ¾ inch.

The *side cutter plier* incorporates the usefulness of the duck bill with the added feature of a rod or wire cutter. The flat serrated jaws can be used to bend or twist small workpieces, while the cutter section is used to cut small rod or wire to required lengths. Pliers of this type are avail-able in lengths of 4 to 8 inches.

[3-8]
locking pliers

Two forms of locking pliers will be discussed in this section. These unique tools supply two features that the previously mentioned forms do not: They can exert far more clamping pressure (up to a ton), and they can

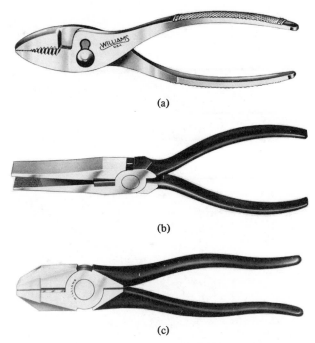

(a)

(b)

(c)

Figure 3-9 — Basic pliers forms. (a) Combination. (b) Duck bill.
(c) Side cutter. *(Courtesy of J.H. Williams, Division of TRW)*

be locked to maintain this pressure, thereby freeing the hand of their user.

Basically, the upper jaw is fixed, while the lower jaw is adjusted with a knurled screw located at the rear end of the tool. The standard procedure for use of the tool is as follows. Squeeze the handles together. Adjust the lower jaw until contact with the workpiece is made. Remove the plier and screw the lower jaw adjust one or two more turns. Place the jaws, with the handles open, over the workpiece and squeeze the handles together to lock the jaws. If more pressure is required, squeeze the release tab located in the handle without the screw, adjust, and rotate another turn or so. Reclamp.

The two locking tools using this principle, shown in Fig. 3-10, are the locking plier wrench and the locking sheet metal plier.

The uses of the locking plier are quite evident in that it is designed to clamp, grip, bend, and twist. The locking sheet metal plier, however, is designed to hold or position one of several sheets of material for such operations as drilling, grinding, or welding. The jaws of this plier are also used to bend or form small sections of sheet metal while maintaining accuracy at the line of bend.

These tools, while rugged, do require that they be kept clean and

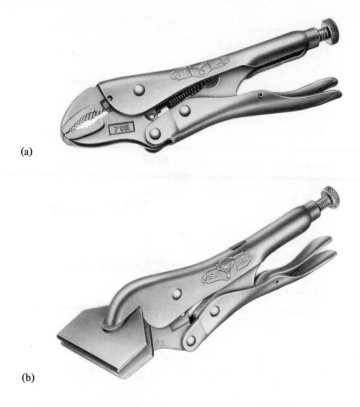

(a)

(b)

Figure 3-10 — (a) Locking pliers. (b) Locking sheet metal pliers. *(Courtesy of Petersen Manufacturing Co.)*

oiled. A drop of oil on the pivot points and thread of the adjusting screw will most certainly increase its life.

[3-9]
screwdrivers, key wrenches

The word *screwdriver* is a term used to describe any of the types of hand tools used to tighten or loosen the various slotted fasteners used in the metal trades. The most often encountered screw fastener head forms are the slotted head screw, the Phillips head screw, and the Allen hex socket screw (Fig. 3-11).

For use with slotted and Phillips head hardware, two main types of

(a) Slot   (b) Phillips   (c) Hexagon

Figure 3-11 — Slotted head types.

screwdrivers are available, the conventional screwdriver and the Phillips screwdriver.

The conventional bladed screwdriver can be obtained in blade widths as small as 0.025 inch to ½ inch or even larger. Screwdrivers are produced in lengths of 3 to 12 inches. Many manufacturers offer a set of six screwdrivers that cover most, if not all, of the screw fastener needs encountered.

The Phillips head screwdriver is recognized by its unique tip design of four flutes with a tip angle of about 30 degrees. This tip is designed to fit into the recessed cross of a Phillips-type screw head. Generally, four sizes are produced: size 1 for the small to number 4 screw, size 2 for a hardware range of 4 through 9, size 3 for a hardware range of 10 to 16 and size 4 for number 18 and larger. Blades from 3 to 12 inches long can be procured.

Screwdrivers are tools used for one specific purpose and should never be used for such operations as prying or shearing. A screwdriver should never be struck by a hammer to impart a force to its tip. Hammer blows to the handle have the effect of chipping the hardened steel work end or can damage and split its handle.

Restoring worn or damaged work tips is normally performed by regrinding. This operation should be performed by a machinist or other qualified person, since poor grinding will damage the temper of the work point.

Allen key wrenches are L-shaped tools of tempered steel whose cross section is that of a hexagon. These tools are designed to fit into the hexagonal recesses of set screws, cap, button, and flat head screws to either tighten or loosen.

Allen keys are produced in sizes that are denoted by the dimension across their hexagonal flat. This range normally includes sizes of 0.028 to 2 inches. Commercial Allen key sets include the following sizes: 0.028, 0.035, 0.050, ⅟₁₆, ⅝₄, ³⁄₃₂, ⅞₄, ⅛, ⁹⁄₆₄, ⁵⁄₃₂, ³⁄₁₆, ⁷⁄₃₂, ¼, and ⁵⁄₁₆ inch.

When the larger sizes of key wrenches are used to tighten hardware, the following procedure is suggested. After inserting the proper key wrench into the screw socket, place the left hand on it so that firm pressure is produced to keep the wrench securely in the hex socket. Maintain this pressure while the right hand either tightens or loosens the hardware. Remember, to keep the hands or knuckles from being scraped, always pull the wrench toward you.

[3-10]
hand shears

Cutting forms from thin sheet metal with either straight or circular cuts most often is performed by the sheet metal hand shear or snips. These tools, made of special heat treated steel, are produced in several forms, as can be seen in Fig. 3-12.

The size of this tool is usually designated by two factors: the length of the cutting jaws and its overall length. Many manufacturers use a number to designate a specific shear size. Be sure to check the actual length and cut before purchasing.

Regular pattern hand shears are used for making straight cuts in sheet metal from a thin to relatively thick gauge. A size range of this type of shear includes a small size number 10 (11½ inches long with a 2½-inch cut) to the larger size number 7 (14½ inches long with a 4-inch cut). This pattern of hand shear is not designed to cut curved or round-shaped edges in sheet metal.

Curved blade pattern shears are designed specifically to cut curved or circular shapes in sheet metal. They are not designed to cut straight lines. The only size available in this pattern is a number 9, 12½ inches long with a 3-inch cut. Curved cuts either to the right or left can be performed with this shear by turning the shear over, so that the curved jaws point in the general direction of the curved layout line.

Combination pattern hand shears are designed to cut both straight or intricate curved lines in sheet metal. The cutting jaw shape is composed of a somewhat lower and rounded form of the regular pattern shear. The range of sizes available in this type include: number 19 (3-inch cut, 12½-inch length), number 18 (3½-inch cut, 13½-inch length) and number 17 (4-inch cut, 14½-inch length).

Compound action hand shears are a group of snips designed to increase the cutting pressure at the shear edge through compound leverage built into the shear frames. This type of shear can be procured in three styles: one that *cuts to the right,* one that *cuts to the left,* and one that *cuts straight or curved.* The purpose of the cuts *right* or *left* types is in the requirement of the technician, be he right- or left-handed. This is important when one is following a layout with hand shears where the jaws may obstruct a visual alignment at the point being cut. The jaws of this type of shear are most often made of molybdenum steel with fine

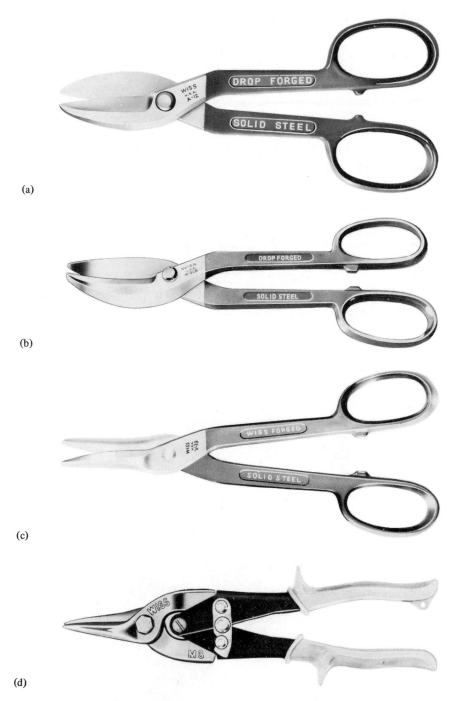

(a)

(b)

(c)

(d)

Figure 3-12 — Hand shears. (a) Regular pattern. (b) Curved pattern. (c) Combination pattern. (d) Compound action. *(Courtesy of J. Wiss & Sons Co.)*

serrations along their cutting edges. These factors, coupled with the increased leverage, result in their ability to cut stainless steel up to 18 gauge in thickness. All three types are made in one size, a 9¾-inch length with a 1⅜-inch cut.

Care of hand shears or snips lies largely in maintaining sharp shearing edges and lubrication at its pivot points. Should nicks or burrs develop along the shear edges, resharpening can be performed with a grinding wheel. Care should be taken to reproduce the original cutting angles. During grinding, the cutting edges should be water-quenched often to keep heat from destroying the temper of the jaws.

[3-11]
hand nibbler

A hand nibbler, Fig. 3-13, is a tool used to nibble or chip holes, slots, or other shapes in sheet steel up to 18 gauge and $\frac{1}{16}$-inch thicknesses in softer metals, such as copper or aluminum. The sole purpose of this tool is to provide cutting action on such items as air ducts, panels, or other finished forms where the use of conventional hand or power tools would prove difficult, because of access.

Figure 3-13 — Hand nibbler. *(Courtesy of Adel Tool Co.)*

The nibbler is a hand-squeeze-powered tool. This power is directed to a hardened chisel-shaped cutter located at the top of the main frame of the tool. When the handle is squeezed, the chisel bit moves toward the chisel face of the handle. This action clamps and nibbles a section of the metal approximately $\frac{1}{4}$ inch wide and $\frac{1}{16}$ inch deep. Release of the handles retracts the chisel punch and allows the work to advance for another cut.

When the need to cut shapes in ducts or centers of flat sheets is encountered, the following procedure is recommended. Punch or drill a hole $\frac{1}{2}$ inch in diameter within the area to be nibbled. Insert the nibbler chisel into the hole and begin the cutting operation.

Care of the nibbler is minimal. Coat moving parts with a good heavy grade of oil. Should the chisel become dull, a replacement can be procured from the manufacturer and installed within a few minutes. After a nibbling operation and prior to storage, remove metal nibs from the tool with a firm bristle brush.

[3-12]
tubing cutters

When tubing is to be cut to a specific length prior to some assembly, a tool called a tubing cutter can be used to perform the task. This tool is shown in Fig. 3-14. The tubing cutter can be used on tube or pipe from $\frac{1}{8}$ inch in diameter up to 2 inches in diameter and larger. Copper, brass, aluminum, gas and water pipe, and thin wall steel tubing fall within the work range of this tool.

The cutting action of this tool is produced with a set of rollers affixed to an adjustable handle that adjusts either in or out. Located and fixed to the tool's main frame is a hardened, thin parting or cutting disc.

In practice, a tube to be cut is placed between the cutting wheel and the adjustable rollers. Pressure is brought to bear on the tube by adjust-

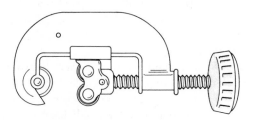

Figure 3-14 — Tubing cutter.

ing the handle until contact pressure is felt. Adjust one-quarter to one-half turn more. Grasp the handle and allow the entire tool to rotate about the pipe or tube. A score mark will be left by the cutting wheel. Adjust the rollers closer and repeat the rotation of the tool until the tube is parted. This tool is extremely useful in removing sections of existing piping when it is necessary to replace or alter its path. For small operations, a tube can be clamped in a bench vise and the cutter located at a specific location.

These tools are denoted by the smallest and largest tube or pipe that they will cut. Sizes of tubing cutters range from $\frac{1}{8}$ to 1 inch, $\frac{5}{8}$ inch to 2 inches, and 2 to 4 inches. Pipe cutters can be procured to cut pipe sizes from $\frac{1}{8}$ inch to 2 inches, from 2 to 4 inches, and from 4 to 6 inches.

Care of tubing cutters requires a cleaning and oiling of rollers, cutter, and threads of the adjusting handle. Should the cutter disc become dull or broken, a new wheel can be installed within a few minutes. A good idea is to have a spare cutter wheel handy for quick replacement.

[3-13]
wrenches

Our discussion of wrenches will be limited to those of basic need to the sheet metal technician. As time and experience dictate, the reader may care to add to this basic set described below.

fixed-size wrenches

Fixed-size wrenches, often called open-end or box wrenches, are by far the most often used type of wrench. These tools are made of high-quality forged steel in one of three basic forms: open end, box end, and combination (Fig. 3-15).

The open-end type is produced so that each end accepts a different size of nut or bolt head. Each end of the wrench has its open end offset 15 degrees from the center line of the tool. This 15-degree offset is extremely useful in tightening or loosening hex-shaped hardware in cramped or close quarters.

The size range of a normal set would include from $\frac{1}{4}$- to $\frac{5}{8}$-inch openings. The smaller range of opening varies by $\frac{1}{16}$-inch increments, while the larger sizes vary by $\frac{1}{8}$-inch increments. A miniature range of these open-end wrenches is available for small hardware and instrument work. This small-sized set normally includes a range from $\frac{13}{64}$ to $\frac{3}{8}$ inch.

Figure 3-15 — Wrenches. (a) Open end. (b) Box end. (c) Combination. *(Courtesy of J.H. Williams, Division of TRW)*

Open-end wrenches are also available in metric sizes that include a range
of 6 to 28 mm.

box wrench

Although the open-end wrench is adequate for all normal work requirements, the box end enhances both turning ability and safety during a
fastening operation. The box wrench, so called because it completely boxes
or surrounds a hex-headed fastener, is made in either a 6-point or 12-
point box.

The points of a box wrench are important, since a 6-point allows
one to make turns in close quarters as small as one-sixth of a full revolution, while the 12-point box allows turns as small as one-twelfth of a
revolution. This is important when one has to make a series of small rota-
tions in a cramped space to either loosen or tighten a fastener. The box
wrench also by its design does not allow the box end to slip off of hardware during an operation, which could hurt or skin the hand of the user.

These tools, as shown in Fig. 3-15, are normally made in the offset
design for both leverage and hand protection. The range of sizes for a

typical set would include ¼ to ¾ inch. Again, as with the open-end wrench, the smaller sizes vary by ¹⁄₁₆-inch increments, while the larger sizes vary by ⅛-inch increments. A miniature set of the box wrench generally includes a size range of ³⁄₁₆ to ¹¹⁄₃₂ inch. Metric-size sets of the box wrench are available in a range of 8 to 32 mm.

The *combination wrench,* so named because it contains both an open end and a box end, is designed to answer two needs. The open end, which is the same size as the box end, is used to rapidly tighten or loosen hardware. When final tightening or initial loosening is reached, the box end is used for both strength and safety. A selection of this type of wrench should include a range of ¼ to ⅝ inch.

[3-14]
adjustable wrenches

Two very common and practical adjustable wrenches that should be in the possession of the technician are the adjustable open-end wrench (Fig. 3-16) and the pipe wrench (not shown).

Figure 3-16 — Adjustable open-end wrench. *(Courtesy of J.H. Williams, Division of TRW)*

adjustable open-end wrench

The adjustable open-end wrench is unique in that the jaw opening on this tool can be varied to accept a wide range of both square- and hex-headed hardware. The upper or fixed jaw is part of the handle, while the lower jaw is adjustable by a rotatable knurled nut within the frame. Some models of this wrench are equipped with a locking plunger, which allows the jaws to be locked to a particular size.

Adjustable wrenches are made of high-quality steel and are available in lengths of 4, 6, 8, 10, 12, and 16 inches. Maximum jaw openings for this group of wrenches ranges from ½ inch to 1¾ inches. The more popular sizes in this wrench are 4 inches and 8 inches.

pipe wrenches

Pipe wrenches are designed to rotate cylindrical shapes, be they rod or pipe. Rotation of a round workpiece by this tool requires that the serrated and hardened jaws of the wrench, dig into the metal.

Both the adjustable or hook jaw and the fixed or heal jaw of this tool are equipped with the hardened *bite* jaws. The adjustable jaw is designed with a floating looseness which allows a more positive bite when pressure is applied to the handle. This floating action is also useful when a new grip area is necessary for tightening. Pressure applied to the handle toward the adjustable jaw will break the grip of the jaws on the round workpiece. Reverse pressure will again lock the jaws to the workpiece.

Pipe wrenches are most commonly available in lengths of 6 to 18 inches with pipe capacities of ⅛ inch to 2 inches.

strap wrenches

The strap wrench, not shown, is a tool used to rotate round workpieces. The strap wrench, however, is designed specifically to be used on workpieces where marring or jaw marks are to be avoided. Clamping and rotation are achieved by a heavy woven cloth strap that encompasses the workpiece and is attached to the handle. The clamping range of this special tool covers a size from ⅛-inch pipe to 2 inches and larger. This tool is one that may be added to the basic set if the work forms encountered require its use.

[3-15]
files

Hardened steel files are used daily to perform operations on metal such as smoothing, removing burrs, forming shapes or slots, or removing excess metal from a workpiece. The cutting action of a file is achieved by a variety of cutting teeth milled or machined into the work face of the file. The shape or style of the teeth is classified according to the way in which the files cut. Figure 3-17 shows the four basic cuts produced in files.

The *single cut* file is so called because its work surface is composed of a series of parallel rows of teeth set at an angle of 60 to 80 degrees to the face edge. The *double cut* file consists of overlapping parallel cuts.

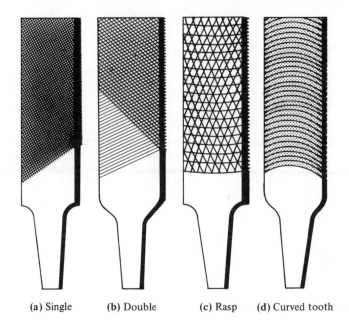

(a) Single　　　(b) Double　　　(c) Rasp　　　(d) Curved tooth

Figure 3-17 — File cuts.

The first cut is usually at an angle of 45 degrees to the work edge, while the second row is set at an angle of 60 to 80 degrees. The *rasp cut* is formed by rows of raised separated teeth. The *curved tooth* file is formed by a series of separate concentric arcs that run the entire work length of the file.

Each file cut is designed to perform specific operations on various materials. The single cut imparts a smooth shaving action to metals; the double cut is used for fast removal of metal. The rasp is designed for use on plastics, wood, or other soft material where large chip clearance is necessary during cutting. The curved tooth file is most often used on soft metals, such as lead or babbit.

Files are further classified by the relative spacing of the rows of teeth. This spacing or coarseness is defined by four levels: coarse, bastard (medium coarse), second cut, and smooth.

Files are produced in various lengths of from 4 to 16 inches in a variety of shapes. The ''shape'' of a file normally refers to its cross-sectional shape; these include rectangular, square, round, half round, and triangular.

Files are made to cut on a forward stroke only. Dragging a file back over a workpiece does nothing but have a dulling effect on the teeth.

Remember—when using a file, always place a wooden file handle over its sharp pointed tang end. Never strike the file with a hammer or attempt to pry with it, as it will fracture.

A useful range of files for a beginning set should include 8- or 10-inch rectangular, square, round, and half round files. A coarse and a second cut type in each shape should prove adequate and fill most needs.

[3-16]
hacksaws

One of the most useful and commonplace tools in the sheet metal trades is the hacksaw. This tool basically consists of a blade frame, hand grip, and a blade tension adjuster. Blades of either 10- or 12-inch lengths can be held within the frame and tightened with the wingnut adjuster located near the handle end of the frame. The blade holder bars, located at each end of the frame, are made in such a way that they will rotate at four positions with respect to the frame. This allows for blades to be positioned to meet special or unique sawing operations.

Hacksaw blades are generally made with teeth-per-inch sizes of 14, 18, 24, and 32. The coarser size teeth are used for large metal sections of $\frac{3}{4}$ inch or thicker. The 18-tooth blade is used for sections of $\frac{1}{4}$ inch to $\frac{3}{4}$ inch. For iron pipe or medium wall tubing, the 24-tooth blade is used. For thin sections of either flat or round stock, the 32-tooth blade is most often used.

When working with a hacksaw, be sure that the teeth always point away from the frame handle. Stand with feet spread forward and backward of your body—this gives balance and motion to the process. Lean forward on the cut stroke and allow the entire blade to work on the piece. At the end of the stroke, remove the pressure on the blade and pull the saw toward you. Press down slightly and push for the next cutting stroke. Never twist the blade during a cut or return stroke, as this can bend and weaken the blade.

review questions

3-1 / List the measuring accuracy generally achieved using the steel tape, the steel scale, and the outside micrometer.

3-2 / What are the decimal values of the following: $\frac{1}{8}$ inch, $\frac{1}{16}$ inch, $\frac{1}{32}$ inch, and $\frac{1}{64}$ inch?

3-3 / Discuss the main uses of the square head and scale and the bevel protractor and scale. What is the measuring accuracy of each?

3-4 / What is the definition of *squaring* as used in the metal trades?

3-5 / With the addition of a vernier scale on a protractor, the accuracy of angular measurement is increased to what fraction of a degree?

3-6 / List the three observations that must be made to determine a decimal size on the outside micrometer.

3-7 / Break each of the following decimal sizes into the three increments as would be denoted on the micrometer: (a) 0.400; (b) 0.299; (c) 0.026; (d) 0.937.

3-8 / Explain "go"—"no go" when gauging a size in wire or sheet.

3-9 / List the basic tools used for scribing lines, etc., on metal.

3-10 / What is the difference between a prick and a center punch? Why is it necessary to have these two punches?

3-11 / A hand chisel is designed to operate on metal in several ways. List them. List the components in a basic set of chisels and describe their uses.

3-12 / Hand pliers are designed to increase gripping power. List the three basic types and the actions they best perform.

3-13 / List the basic styles of hand pattern shears and their specific purposes.

3-14 / What is the main purpose of the hand held nibbler?

3-15 / Describe the procedure used in cutting a length of tubing with a tubing cutter.

3-16 / List two points that make the box wrench a most popular tool.

3-17 / What is the purpose of the combination wrench?

3-18 / What two forms of adjustable wrenches are in common use? How do they differ?

3-19 / List the four basic cuts available in hand files. What further definition to a file cut can be listed?

3-20 / When installing a blade in a hand hacksaw, how must the teeth be positioned?

3-21 / Hacksaw blades are graded by the teeth per inch. List the four more common types available.

4

basics of layout

[4-1]
introduction

The previous chapters of this text were presented as a basic foundation
for an understanding of metals and some of their important characteristics. Often commercial products used in fabrications such as tubing,
angle, or bar stock are used as shaped, with only the length being altered.
Sheet metal and thin plates, however, have many operations performed
on them prior to a finished state. Flat metal sheets may have holes, both
round or rectangular, produced in them prior to being formed into such
items as covers, brackets, or frames for mounting electrical or mechanical

assemblies. Frames that serve as mounting containers for such items are called *chassis*.

Most often, prints or sketches, giving the dimensions of the formed piece, are supplied. The overall finished dimensions of the formed piece are shown, as well as the location of holes, round, square, or rectangular. These specifics are portrayed on what are called "views" of the workpiece.

Let us delay the discussion of the means and methods of producing the holes and concentrate on the sheet metal drawing itself.

[4-2]
sheet metal drawings

The responsibility for laying out and producing a single metal form or a series of metal forms often fall on the shoulders of the sheet metal technician. This product may be a one of a kind or the beginning of a new product, often called a *prototype*. It is essential for the technician to perform this vital task with foreknowledge of both tools and techniques.

Let us look at a single-view sheet metal drawing, as shown in Fig. 4-1.

A drawing or sketch is your guide to producing the part as specified by the draftsman. The format of a good drawing will detail the following information.

1 / Material—type and thickness.

2 / Number of pieces required.

3 / The tolerance range of overall form, of hole sizes and of their locations.

4 / Dimensioned locations of all holes with sizes indicated.

5 / Installation of hardware such as nuts, studs, etc.

6 / Final treatment of the finished part; that is, painting, irriditing, anodizing, graining, etc.

The treatment and hardware types encountered in sheet metal will be discussed in detail at a later time.

Generally, the first three items mentioned above are found in the lower right-hand corner of the drawing or print. This block, called a "title block" contains the information basic to the beginning of the workpiece.

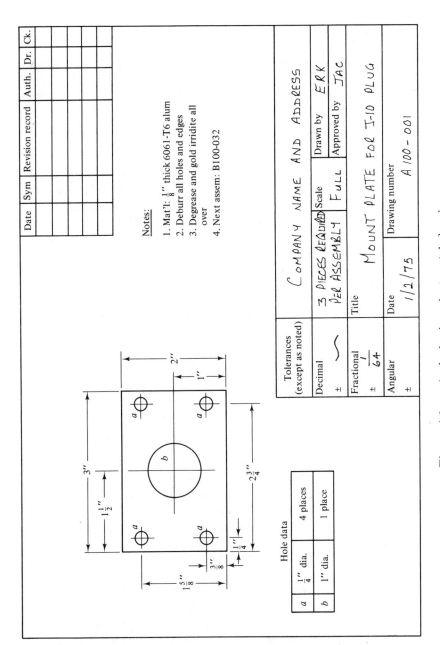

Figure 4-1 — A single-view sheet metal drawing.

The actual shape of the workpiece is shown, in either a full-scale or scaled-down version, over the remaining print.

In standard practice, flat workpieces, those that have no bends or curved surfaces, are represented in a single top view with its thickness not shown. When a workpiece has bends or holes, or hardware located on those bent sections, extra views are shown so that the holes or punchings can be dimensioned. This form of drawing can be seen in Fig. 4-2. It is called an *orthographic projection.*

Orthographic projections or drawings are used as a standard practice to detail the various faces or viewing planes of a workpiece. This form is used where a workpiece has dimensions of length, width, and depth and where specific locations of holes, slots, bends, etc. are noted.

To understand the method and reasoning of orthographic projections, let us consider a dice cube. This cube has six faces that, while they are of the same size, contain various number patterns of dots (one to six). In describing this unique pattern of dots on the cube to a friend who has never seen one, you attempt to show it on a drawing. He, by the way, understands orthographic projection. In showing the six faces and the dot relations you find you must show six views or faces. The views also must be arranged so that the dots will appear in their proper positions and so that mating faces are in agreement. Holding the die in your hands, you pick the face with the one dot to start and call it the *top view.* To better understand this process, refer to Fig. 4-3.

The cube is now resting on a table, and the second face chosen is called the *front view.* Looking directly at this second view, we describe the pattern in the second drawing and call it the *front view.* Moving to the right side of the cube on the table, we look directly at its face and draw it. This view of the right face is called the *right side view.* This is repeated with the left and rear faces with resulting *left* and *rear views.* To show the bottom face of the cube, as it sits on the table, rotate the top face of the die away from you until the bottom face is in the top position. This pattern can be drawn and called the *bottom view.* The drawings with the six faces denoted would be immediately understood by your friend. If you gave him dimensions and locations of the various holes on the dice cube, he could produce a model.

Really, that is the function of an orthographic drawing. It is intended to give you the dimensions of length and width, and the hole locations on the various face views of a workpiece.

In most cases, three views are sufficient to detail a workpiece. These views are *top view, front view,* and *right side view.* Other views would be used if needed to detail operations, holes, slots, etc. on particular surfaces.

Dimensions shown in good drawing form are referenced from two 90-degree intersecting lines or sides of the part. These reference sides

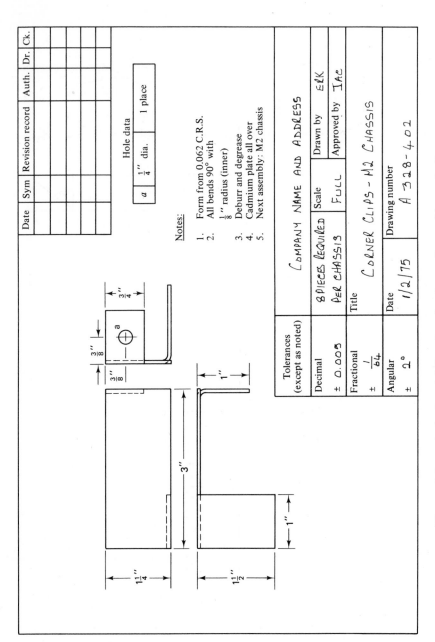

Figure 4-2 — A sheet metal drawing showing orthographic projection.

The following appears within the drawing:

Date	Sym	Revision record	Auth.	Dr.	Ck.

Hole data

	dia.	1 place
a	$\frac{1}{4}$"	

Notes:

1. Form from 0.062 C.R.S.
2. All bends 90° with $\frac{1}{8}$" radius (inner)
3. Deburr and degrease
4. Cadmium plate all over
5. Next assembly: M2 chassis

COMPANY NAME AND ADDRESS

Tolerances (except as noted)		Scale	Drawn by	ELK
Decimal ± 0.005	8 PIECES REQUIRED PER CHASSIS	FULL	Approved by	IAc
Fractional ± $\frac{1}{64}$	Title CORNER CLIPS - M2 CHASSIS			
Angular ± 2°	Date 1/2/75	Drawing number A 328-402		

$\frac{3}{4}$" $\frac{3}{8}$" $\frac{3}{8}$"   a

3"   1"   1" $1\frac{1}{4}$" $1\frac{1}{2}$"

67

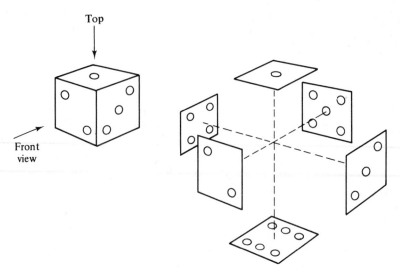

(a) Dice cubes with face planes

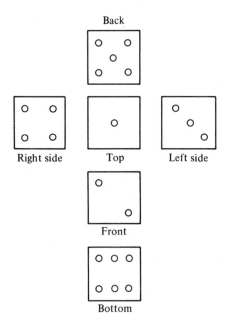

(b) Orthographic projections of the faces
of a dice cube

Figure 4-3 — A dice cube.

are normally the left and bottom edge of the view. Thus, dimensions are read from left to right and from bottom to top to locate a point or line.

[4-3]
precision sheet metal tolerances

Within the machine tool trades, finished pieces can be produced having dimensions within tolerances of ±0.001 inch and closer. This means that dimensions such as diameters, location, shape, and depths are within 0.001 inch of the specified dimensions given on the print.

Consider a dimension such as $10\frac{3}{4}$ inches ($\pm\frac{1}{32}$ inch). This states that if you locate that dimension exactly at the $10\frac{3}{4}$-(10.750-)-inch mark, you have placed it perfectly. The tolerance range ($\pm\frac{1}{32}$ inch) means that you can locate the dimension with the range of $\frac{1}{32}$ of an inch before or after the main dimension of $10\frac{3}{4}$. Thus, the range of the tolerance is $10\frac{23}{32}$ (10.718) inches to $10\frac{25}{32}$ (10.781) inches. A point or dimension located within this range is said to "be in tolerance."

Precision sheet metal forms can and are produced routinely with length, widths, and depth dimensions within $\pm\frac{1}{32}$ inch of a given dimension. In some instances, tolerance ranges of $\pm\frac{1}{64}$ (0.015) inch are achieved.

In the production of the various required hole shapes, using modern equipment, the size of the holes and their placement can be sized and located within ±0.005 inch of the main dimension.

To summarize, the normal tolerance range of formed sheet metal parts is generally taken to be within $\pm\frac{1}{32}$ inch. Some instances require tolerances of $\pm\frac{1}{64}$ inch. This is called precision sheet metal forming.

[4-4]
basic layout tools

The techniques described in the following text are presented to aid the reader in producing precision layouts when such procedures are required. The basic tools necessary for this work are a steel scriber; a rigid steel scale with graduations of $\frac{1}{4}$, $\frac{1}{8}$, $\frac{1}{16}$, $\frac{1}{32}$ and $\frac{1}{64}$ inch (the length of the scale is generally 18 or 24 inches long); a 6- or 8-inch divider, used to draw circles or arcs, or to space off lengths along a line; and a square head, bevel protractor, and grooved scale used to locate points and lines, and to produce lines at specific angles to a given line or edge.

The most common use of the square head and adjustable scale is in locating the placement dimension of a hole center or a line. In the case of a cut or sheared sheet, the locating dimension of a hole or a line is set on the adjustable scale and locked. The machined surface of the square head is held firmly in contact with the reference edge of the sheet, and a mark is produced by a scriber at the proper setting. The scale is then reset to the second locating dimension. The square head is placed at the second reference edge. A second scribed line is ruled so that it intersects the first line. This is the location of the required point.

The bevel protractor is used in combination with the scale to produce angles other than 90 degrees. Bevel protractors with vernier scales can produce angles within an accuracy of one-fourth of a degree (15 minutes). This was described earlier.

[4-5]
basic constructions

parallel lines

Parallel lines to an existing line may be constructed with extreme accuracy by using the following technique. Determine the spacing or dimension that exists between the parallel lines, and set a divider to that dimension. Place one point of the divider on the given line and scribe an arc in the direction of the required line. Move some distance from this point along the same base line and perform the construction of a second arc. Lay a scale about the scribed arcs so that they both align with the edge of the scale; then scribe a line. The scribed line is now parallel to the original line. This same technique can be extended to producing more than one parallel line.

construction of a right angle or perpendicular to a given point

In the layout of many geometric figures such as squares, rectangles, etc., it is often necessary to construct lines at right angles to an existing line.

Figure 4-4 shows two constructions that are frequently used: *a perpendicular to some point located on the line* and *a perpendicular at the end point of a line.*

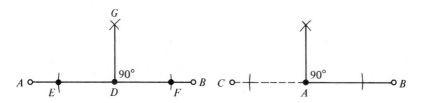

Figure 4-4 — Perpendicular constructions.

To construct a line perpendicular to a point D located on some line AB, the following procedure is recommended. Using a compass set at some convenient radius r and the point D as the center, scribe arcs so that they intersect the main line AB at some points E and F. Increasing the radius previously set on the compass and using the points E and F now as centers, produce arcs from each so that they intersect at some point G. A line drawn between point G and the original point D is at an angle of 90 degrees to the existing the line AB and at the point required.

To construct a perpendicular to an end point of a line, the afore-mentioned method can be employed. Consider the need to produce a line perpendicular to line AB at point A. The first step is to extend the line AB so some point C. Choosing some convenient radius on the compass, and using point A as its center, scribe arcs so as to intersect the line AB and its extension. Using these arc-line intersections as new centers, scribe intersecting arcs. A line drawn from this intersection to the original point A forms a line perpendicular to AB.

to bisect a given line

To bisect a given line requires a simple two-step approach. Using the end points of the line AB as centers (see Fig. 4-5), set a compass so that arcs produced from these end points, above and below the line, intersect each

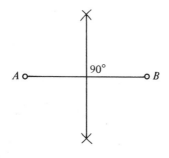

Figure 4-5 — Bisection of a line.

other. A line constructed from these arc intersections both bisects the given line *AB* and is perpendicular to the given line.

to construct an angle of 45 degrees to a given point on a line

Given some line *AB* with point *C* located on it, an angle of 45 degrees is to be constructed at point *C*. Figure 4-6 graphically illustrates the following procedure. In the direction in which the 45-degree angle is to be constructed, locate some point *D* a convenient distance from the required angle vertex, point *C*. At this point *D*, erect a line *ND* perpendicular to the line *AB*. Using a radius equal to the distance *CD*, and point *D* as a center, draw an arc so that it passes through point *C* and intersects line *ND* at some point *M*. A line drawn from point *M* to *C* is thus at an angle of 45 degrees to the given line *AB* at point *C*.

the equally spaced location of points along a given line length or between a given line length

Very often, the technician is required to locate a specified number of equally spaced points along a given line length. This may occur in laying out positions for a row of electrical switches on a control panel or in locating a series of holes for the even spacing of screws, rivets, or other types of hardware on a workpiece.

To perform this task, two facts must be known: the *length of the line* on which the positions must be located, and the *total number of points* to be located over a given length or between a given length. As shown in Fig. 4-7, points can be evenly spaced over a full line length or spaced within a line length.

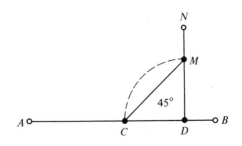

Figure 4-6 — Construction of a 45° angle.

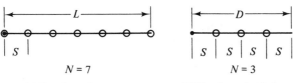

$N = 7$

(a) Equal spacing over a given length L

$N = 3$

(b) Equal spacing between a given length D

Figure 4-7 — Determining equal spacing.

In situations where *spacing* is performed *over a full line length,* the following equation is presented.

$$S = \frac{L}{N-1} \qquad [4\text{--}1]$$

where

$S =$ spacing from point to point

$L =$ overall length of line

$N-1 =$ number of points minus 1

When *spacings* must be performed *between a given length or space,* Eq. [4-2] is used.

$$S = \frac{D}{N+1} \qquad [4\text{--}2]$$

where

$S =$ spacing from point to point

$D =$ distance that points are to be located within

$N+1 =$ number of points plus 1

construction of a rectangle or square if their dimensions are given

The construction procedures are identical for the layout of both the rectangle and the square. The following description and illustration have been applied to the rectangle, as this is the more often encountered situation.

Given two lines of different length, AB and AC (Fig. 4-8), select the longer of the two, line AB, and make this the base of the rectangle. At each end point of the line AB, erect a line perpendicular to it. Set the compass to a length equal to the line AC. Using both points A and B as centers, strike arcs, as shown in Fig. 4-8, intersecting the previously erected perpendiculars. Scribe a line between these two points C, D, thus constructing the rectangle $ACDB$.

bolt pattern layout

Circular bolt pattern layouts on panels or flanges are often encountered, and a thorough understanding of the following procedure will prove invaluable to the technician.

Evenly spaced bolt patterns are normally called out on a drawing in one of several methods. One form, as an illustration, states: *6 equally spaced holes located on a 4¾-inch diameter bolt circle—drilled ¼ inch through.* The second form, abbreviated and denoted on a drawing, shows the above as: ⑥ *¼-inch holes on a 4¾ equally spaced D.B.C.* The letters D.B.C. merely stand for diameter bolt circle.

With the use of a divider, scale, and Table 4-1, one can accurately lay out equal circular hole patterns from three to 100 spaces. Let us return to our above spacing problem and pursue it to final layout.

Since the D.B.C. is 4¾ inches, set your divider to the radius of this circle (2⅜ inches). Place the point of the divider at the center location of the bolt pattern and scribe a circle. The second step requires that you use the table of constants shown in Table 4-1.

Look down the column marked "No. of spaces" until you find 6. Immediately to the right is a value called the "length of chord" constant. In the case of six spaces, the value is 0.5000. Multiplying the diameter of the bolt circle by this constant, you have:

$$4.750 \times 0.500 = 2.375 \ (2⅜ \text{ inch})$$

This value is the chord length between each of the six even spaces of the 4¾-inch bolt circle. Set the dividers to this value and place one point on the circumference of the drawn circle of Fig. 4-9.

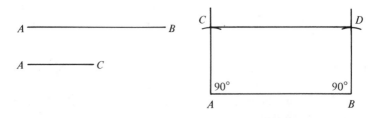

Figure 4-8 — Construction of a rectangle, given two sides.

Table 4-1
LENGTH OF CHORD CONSTANTS *

No. of spaces	Length of chord	No. of spaces	Length of chord
3	0.866025	51	0.061560
4	0.707106	52	0.060378
5	0.587785	53	0.059240
6	0.500000	54	0.058144
7	0.433883	55	0.057088
8	0.382683	56	0.056070
9	0.342020	57	0.055087
10	0.309017	58	0.054138
11	0.281732	59	0.053222
12	0.258819	60	0.052336
13	0.239315	61	0.051478
14	0.222520	62	0.050649
15	0.207911	63	0.049845
16	0.195090	64	0.049067
17	0.183749	65	0.048313
18	0.173648	66	0.047581
19	0.164594	67	0.046872
20	0.156434	68	0.046183
21	0.149042	69	0.045514
22	0.142314	70	0.044864
23	0.136166	71	0.044233
24	0.130526	72	0.043619
25	0.125333	73	0.043022
26	0.120536	74	0.042441
27	0.116092	75	0.041875
28	0.111964	76	0.041324
29	0.108118	77	0.040788
30	0.104528	78	0.040265
31	0.101168	79	0.039756
32	0.098017	80	0.039259
33	0.095056	81	0.038775
34	0.092268	82	0.038302
35	0.089639	83	0.037841
36	0.087155	84	0.037391
37	0.084805	85	0.036951
38	0.082579	86	0.036522
39	0.080466	87	0.036102
40	0.078459	88	0.035692
41	0.076549	89	0.035291
42	0.074730	90	0.034899
43	0.072995	91	0.034516
44	0.071339	92	0.034141
45	0.069756	93	0.033774
46	0.068242	94	0.033414
47	0.066792	95	0.033063
48	0.065403	96	0.032719
49	0.064070	97	0.032381
50	0.062790	98	0.032051
		99	0.031727
		100	0.031410

* For circles of other diameters, multiply length given in the table by the diameter of the circle.

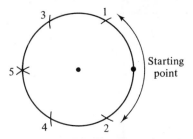

Figure 4-9 — A circular bolt pattern layout.

Strike arc intersections about either side of this point (1, 2). Use the intersections 1 and 2 as new centers to produce two more intersections (3, 4). Finally, with 3 and 4 as centers, strike intersecting arcs, producing 5. Whenever the above process of hole layout is performed, always maintain the "two-direction" layout pattern. This will tend to eliminate error buildup in divider settings. If you continued in only one direction for the spacing layout, you would find that the last space would be, in general, poorly spaced to the beginning point.

[4-6]
bending allowance
introduction

The bending of a section of sheet metal to some angular position with respect to the remaining section may seem rather straightforward at first, but let us consider the possible variations of the actual bend.

Due to both the characteristics and required manufactured form, a bend may exist in many forms. Figure 4-10 illustrates some of the more common types encountered.

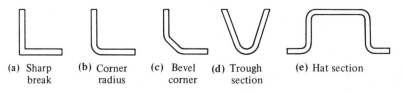

(a) Sharp break (b) Corner radius (c) Bevel corner (d) Trough section (e) Hat section

Figure 4-10 — Common bend types.

Of the five bend sections shown in Fig. 4-10, the sharp break corner is normally used on very thin ductile sheets. The use of this sharp bend is not recommended, since the bend line along this corner is very weak, particularly when metals in the temper state are used. Fracture lines often develop, and over varying periods of time the bent section will physically part.

The remaining four sections are designed for strength as well as appearance of the finished product. It should be obvious that each has a curve or radius that forms the bend shape.

We can now discuss two forces that are created whenever a ductile metal piece is bent or flexed. These forces are *tension* and *compression*. Figure 4-11 shows the location and results of these forces on a bent section of metal. As a metal section is being formed to some inner radius R, the metal along surface A must be compacted or *compressed* to allow the formation of the final section. The metal along surface B at the bend line must stretch to allow forming the final section. This stretching of a material is called *tension force*. The point of this discussion is that in any deformation or bending, both forces, tension and compression, are present. When tension forces are greater than the tensile strength of the material, a fracture or crack will form.

[4-7]
bend allowance

Let us now assume that we are to construct two metal sections, a sharp break and one with a corner radius, using 0.005-inch thick aluminum sheet.

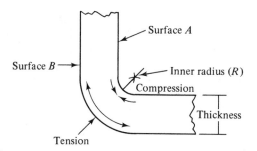

Figure 4-11 — Forces present in bending.

Both sections are to have the same height and base dimensions. The inner radius at the corner is ½ (0.500) inch. See Fig. 4-12.

Both sections naturally will be first cut from flat sheet of proper length and width. The flat layouts, often called "stretchouts," are then formed into their required shape. In the case of section A, Fig. 4-12, one could produce a section within tolerance by adding the lengths of the two legs and arrive at a flat section 3 inches + 3 inches = 6 inches wide. Being thin and having a sharp break, the formed section would be produced in tolerance.

Section B, however, is a different problem. To calculate a flat layout, one would have to perform a calculation somewhat along the lines of the following.

First, we determine the amount or length of metal used in forming the ½-inch radius. Since the radiused section is a 90-degree form, we calculate the circumference of a whole circle with a radius of ½ inch. Cir = πD or Cir = 3.1416 × 1 = 3.1416 inches. Since we are using only one-fourth of the full circumference to produce the radius, the metal length required is 3.1416 ÷ 4 = 0.785 inch or $^{25}\!/_{32}$ inch. Adding to this the two remaining straight sections, each of which is 2½ inches long, we have a total stretchout equal to: 0.785 + 2.500 + 2.500 = 5.785 inches, or $5^{25}\!/_{32}$ inches. It should be obvious that less metal is used to produce section B, although each has the same height and base dimensions.

The above presentation was made to introduce the reader to an important step in preparing a flat sheet stretchout that is sized so that, when it is formed, it will produce both the required shape and dimensions specified on a drawing.

Calculating allowances for sheet metal bends is a most important factor and the reader should make a strong effort to comprehend it before embarking on any project.

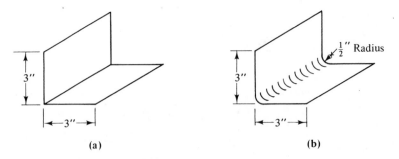

Figure 4-12 — Metal sections with (a) a sharp break and (b) a corner radius.

[4-8]
ninety-degree bends

Bends of 90 degrees will often be performed in material of various tempers and thicknesses, and the above approach *will not* give accurate results.

To aid the reader in determining the flat lengths of sheet metal required to form a given radius, let us look at a basic equation.

$$L = (2 - \frac{\pi}{2})r - (2 - \frac{\pi}{2}K)t$$

where

$L =$ flat length of material to produce the 90-degree radius

$r =$ inner radius of the bend

$K =$ constant

$t =$ thickness of the metal

All of the above variables can be ascertained from the drawing or print describing the bend joint, as, for example, Fig. 4-2. The constant K, however, can and does vary according to the various metal strengths and compositions. This constant K, through experimental evaluation, has been found to range in values of 0.333, 0.40, to 0.5.

The general values for K are commonly taken as ⅓ for mild steels where bends are made against the grain and ½ for bends where the radius is greater than twice the thickness of the material. The general form of the equation for determining allowances for 90-degree bends is thus:

$$L = R\,(0.429) + T(2 - \frac{\pi}{2}K) \qquad [4\text{-}3]$$

where

$L =$ flat length of stock to produce a given radiused 90-degree bend

$R =$ inner radius of bend

$T =$ material thickness

$K = 0.333$ for mild steel against grain bends

$K = 0.5$ for bends where the radius is greater than twice the thickness of the material.

[NOTE]

The value of **K** can vary other than the above given values. This would have to be determined from test bends.

Restating Eq. [4-3] into its forms using both K values, we have

$$L = R(0.429) + T(1.215) \qquad [4\text{-}4]$$

where K factor is 0.5.

$$L = R(0.429) + T(1.48) \qquad [4\text{-}5]$$

where K factor is 0.3.

To aid the reader in determining the bend allowance for various radii and thicknesses, Table 4-2 is offered. This table of values can be used with reasonable accuracy in forming cold rolled steel, half hard brass, and half hard aluminum.

To illustrate the above equations, let us return to Fig. 4-12(b). We had assumed a soft aluminum sheet of 0.005-inch thickness with an inner radius of ½ inch. Our previous rough calculation of the length of metal used to form the radius was 0.785. Using Eq. [4-4], solve for L:

$$L = 0.5(0.429) + 0.005(1.215) \qquad [4\text{-}4]$$

$$= 0.214 + 0.006$$

$$= 0.220 \text{ inch}$$

This large difference is due to a theoretical versus a practical equation. The L value of 0.220 is the correct value.

[4-9]
bends other than
90 degrees

Sheet metal forms, due to design, often contain bends that are either greater or less than the more common 90-degree type. Figure 4-13 shows some of these types and their degrees noted in proper form.

Calculating the length L of the material to produce a bend other than 90 degrees makes use of the equations given for 90-degree bends,

Table 4-2
BEND ALLOWANCE FOR 90° BENDS

B.W.GA	$\frac{1}{32}$	$\frac{3}{64}$	$\frac{1}{16}$	$\frac{5}{64}$	$\frac{3}{32}$	$\frac{7}{64}$	$\frac{1}{8}$	$\frac{9}{64}$	$\frac{5}{32}$	$\frac{11}{64}$	$\frac{3}{16}$	$\frac{13}{64}$	$\frac{7}{32}$	$\frac{15}{64}$	$\frac{1}{4}$	$\frac{9}{32}$	$\frac{5}{16}$	$\frac{11}{32}$	$\frac{3}{8}$	$\frac{7}{16}$	$\frac{1}{2}$
.300																	.499	.512	.525	.549	.579
.284																.466	.479	.492	.506	.529	.559
.259															.422	.435	.449	.462	.476	.499	.529
.238														.390	.396	.410	.423	.437	.450	.473	.504
.220													.361	.368	.374	.388	.401	.415	.428	.451	.482
.203												.333	.340	.347	.354	.367	.381	.394	.408	.431	.461
.180											.299	.306	.313	.319	.326	.339	.353	.366	.379	.403	.433
.165										.274	.281	.288	.294	.301	.308	.321	.335	.348	.361	.385	.415
.148									.247	.254	.260	.267	.273	.280	.287	.300	.314	.327	.340	.364	.394
.134								.223	.230	.237	.243	.250	.257	.263	.270	.283	.297	.310	.324	.347	.377
.120							.199	.206	.213	.220	.226	.233	.240	.246	.253	.266	.280	.293	.307	.330	.360
.109						.179	.186	.193	.199	.206	.213	.220	.226	.233	.240	.253	.263	.276	.293	.317	.347
.095					.156	.162	.169	.176	.182	.189	.200	.203	.209	.216	.223	.236	.250	.263	.276	.300	.330
.083				.135	.141	.148	.154	.161	.169	.175	.181	.188	.195	.201	.208	.222	.235	.245	.262	.285	.314
.072			.114	.121	.128	.134	.141	.148	.155	.161	.172	.178	.181	.188	.195	.208	.222	.235	.248	.272	.302
.065		.100	.106	.113	.119	.126	.133	.139	.146	.153	.164	.166	.173	.180	.186	.200	.213	.226	.240	.263	.293
.058	.084	.092	.098	.104	.111	.117	.124	.131	.138	.144	.155	.158	.164	.171	.178	.191	.205	.218	.231	.255	.285
.049	.073	.081	.087	.093	.100	.107	.113	.120	.127	.133	.144	.147	.153	.160	.167	.180	.194	.207	.220	.244	.274
.042	.065	.072	.078	.084	.091	.098	.105	.111	.118	.125	.136	.138	.145	.152	.158	.172	.185	.198	.212	.235	.266
.035	.056	.064	.070	.076	.083	.090	.096	.103	.110	.116	.127	.130	.136	.143	.150	.163	.177	.190	.203	.227	.257
.032	.053	.060	.066	.072	.079	.086	.093	.099	.106	.113	.119	.126	.133	.139	.146	.160	.173	.186	.200	.223	.253
.028	.048	.055	.061	.068	.074	.081	.088	.094	.101	.108	.114	.121	.128	.135	.141	.155	.168	.182	.195	.218	.249
.025	.044	.052	.057	.064	.071	.077	.084	.091	.097	.104	.111	.118	.124	.131	.138	.151	.164	.178	.191	.214	.245
.022	.040	.048	.054	.060	.067	.074	.080	.087	.094	.100	.107	.114	.121	.127	.134	.147	.161	.174	.188	.211	.241
.020	.038	.045	.051	.058	.065	.071	.078	.085	.091	.098	.104	.111	.118	.125	.132	.145	.158	.172	.185	.208	.239
.018	.035	.043	.049	.055	.062	.069	.076	.082	.089	.096	.102	.109	.116	.122	.129	.143	.156	.169	.183	.206	.236

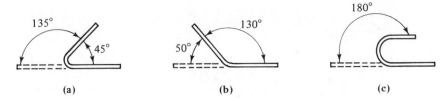

Figure 4-13 — Bend notation.

with but one more operation. This one additional operation is the multi-plication of the value L by the value obtained from the division of the required angle by 90 degrees.

[NOTE]

The required angle is the angle through which the material moves to produce the bend. Thus, in Fig. 4-13(a), the material must move through an angle (180 — 45 degrees) = 135 degrees, while in (b) it must move through (180 — 130 degrees) = 50 degrees.

Let us illustrate this operation on the bend section shown in Fig. 4-14. Gathering specified facts, we see that two bends are specified: 180 degrees with a R of ⅝ inch (0.625 inch) and a 45-degree bend with R of ¼ inch (0.250 inch). The material is ⅛-inch (0.125-inch) thick and in the soft state. Using Eq. [4-4], we may now calculate the L for each bend.

$$L(180°) = 0.625(0.429) + T(1.215) \times {}^{180}\!/_{90}$$

$$L(180°) = (0.268 + 0.152) \times 2$$

$$L(180°) = 0.840 \text{ inch}$$

$$L(45°) = 0.250(0.429) + (0.125)(1.215) \times {}^{135}\!/_{90}$$

$$L(45°) = (0.107 + 0.152)1.5$$

$$L(45°) = 0.258 \times 1.5 = 0.388 \text{ inch}$$

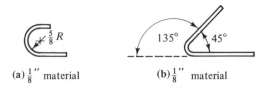

(a) ⅛″ material   (b) ⅛″ material

Figure 4-14

Referring back to our bend allowance table for ⅛-inch material with a 0.250-inch radius, we see a bend value of 0.253 inch. This allowance is for a 90-degree bend. To produce our angle of 45 degrees, material had to be bent an additional 45 degrees, which resulted in an L of 0.388.

[4-10]
stretchout development

Developing a stretchout from an actual section or drawing is the daily task of the sheet metal technician. This process is one of determining the length and width of a flat sheet that when formed will produce the form and required dimensions of the workpiece.

The development of a stretchout's length and/or width is a relatively simple operation when understood.

In essence, a two-step operation is performed, one of addition and one of subtraction. To understand the working of this process, let us refer to Fig. 4-15.

The three dimensioned sections shown in Fig. 4-15 are an *unequal-*

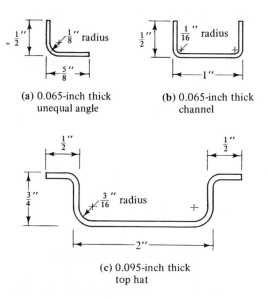

(a) 0.065-inch thick
unequal angle

(b) 0.065-inch thick
channel

(c) 0.095-inch thick
top hat

Figure 4-15

legged angle, a *channel,* and a *hat section.* Let us develop the stretchout length for each of the sections shown.

The first step in any length development is the addition of all the section's sides, *only the outside dimensions* being used. In the case of the angle, the sum of the outside dimensions is

$$\tfrac{1}{2} + \tfrac{5}{8} = 1\tfrac{1}{8}$$

We now must look at the figure for the number of bends and their radius. The thickness must also be noted. In the unequal-angle section, we have one radius bend with a value equal to a $\tfrac{1}{8}$-inch R. The final step in our determination of the stretchout length requires that we subtract the bend allowance for each bend from the outside summation of its sides. We have one radius. Consulting the tables for 90-degree bends, we find that a $\tfrac{1}{8}$-inch radius bend in 0.065-inch thick material requires 0.133 inch to form. Thus, the final stretchout length for this section is

$$1.125 - 0.133 = 0.992 \text{ inch}$$

Performing the above operation on the channel and the top hat section, we have the following stretchout lengths.

Channel —

$$\textit{Outside summation} = \tfrac{1}{2} + 1 + \tfrac{1}{2} = 2.00$$
$$\text{One bend allowance } L = 0.106$$

Since two such bends are used, *total bend allowance* is $0.106 \times 2 = 0.212$. *Stretchout length* is therefore

$$2.00 - 0.212 = 1.788 \text{ inches}$$

Top Hat —

$$\textit{Outside summation} = \tfrac{1}{2} + \tfrac{3}{4} + 2 + \tfrac{3}{4} + \tfrac{1}{2} = 4\tfrac{1}{2}$$

Total bend allowance is $4 \times 0.200 = 0.800$. *Stretchout length* is therefore

$$4.500 - 0.800 = 3.700 \text{ inches}$$

In some drawings, the thickness of the metal must be added to a dimension to obtain the true outside dimension of a particular side. Always be sure that the outside dimension of a leg is truly the total outside dimension.

[4-11]
procedures in
stretchout layout

Once the stretchout dimensions of a workpiece have been determined, its layout on a flat sheet can begin. Since we have previously worked the flat length requirements of the sections shown in Fig. 4-15, let us show them in flat form patterns.

The unequal angle section was calculated to have a flat length of 0.992 inch. Let us assume that the length of the formed angle is to be 2 inches. Our flat sheet to produce the angle now has a length of 2 inches and a stretchout width of 0.992 inch. The layout of lines begins at the left side of our piece, shown in Fig. 4-16.

Let us begin our layout of the ½-inch leg. Scribe a line ½ inch in from the left end of the pattern. This is noted as A-A in our figure. From previous calculations, we now know that a bend allowance of 0.133 is required to produce the required radius. Using line A-A, scribe a parallel line B-B toward the left end of the pattern equal to 0.133. This bend allowance strip is shown shaded in our figure.

During any pattern layout, you must scribe in the allowance strip, since this allowance strip is mutually used by both legs in their formation. The second leg (⅝ inch) is measured from the line B-B of the bend allowance strip. The stretchout patterns of the channel and top hat are also shown in Fig. 4-16.

One final note before we begin our next section. Locations of holes or other shapes that are required must be placed on the pattern before forming. This is important for the various operations necessary prior to bending. Suppose we were required to place a ½-inch diameter hole centered on the 2-inch long section of our top hat. This position line would be measured from the same reference line used to measure the 2-inch span. For a central location, we would locate a line 1 inch from the reference line used to measure the 2-inch span.

The allowance strips, other than their importance in developing a pattern layout, are of prime importance when the pattern is placed in a machine for bending. It gives a visual alignment of the zone to be radiused with the forming tool.

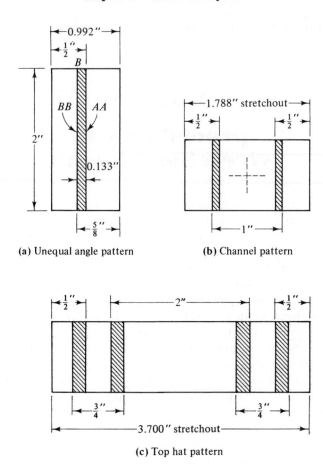

(a) Unequal angle pattern   (b) Channel pattern

(c) Top hat pattern

Figure 4-16 — Pattern layout.

[4-12]
box pan layout

A box pan is a form having a square or rectangular shape with an attached bottom. The top is generally omitted or can be attached independently at a later time. This simple form is used most often in chassis forms, metal chests, and liquid holding tanks.

The flat layout or stretchout for the pan box must start with the length and width of the flat sheet to produce the final shape. This is performed by addition of the outside dimensions in both its length and width. Should the box pan have hems, corner radii, flanges, or other features, they must be calculated into the stretchout. Figure 4-17 is illustrative of a simple box layout.

This box is basic in that there are no corner radii, hems, or corner folds. Thus, its stretchout is shown [Fig. 4-17(b)] with fold lines dotted. Ninety-degree folds along the dotted lines would result in the pan box shown in Fig. 4-17(a).

Suppose that the box shown in Fig. 4-17 was made of $\frac{1}{16}$-inch thick half hard aluminum and had corner radii equal to $\frac{1}{8}$ inch. The stretchout would be different from that shown in Fig. 4-17(b) due to the bend allowances required to form the corners.

Let us look at the 12-inch wide section of the box and compute the material to form this section of the box. This section is shown in Fig. 4-18.

First, we add up the outside dimensions of this view:

1 / $4 + 12 + 4 = 20$ inches (no radius bend)

2 / Two $\frac{1}{8}$-inch bends in $\frac{1}{16}$-inch thick material are used in this section; the bend allowance is thus

$$L = (0.429 \times 0.125) + (0.062 \times 1.48)$$
$$L = 0.053 + 0.091$$
$$L = 0.145 \text{ inch}$$
$$2L = 0.290 \text{ inch}$$

or

3 / Subtracting the two bend allowances from line 1, we have a calculated stretchout

$$L = 20 - 0.290$$
$$L = 19.709 \text{ inches}$$

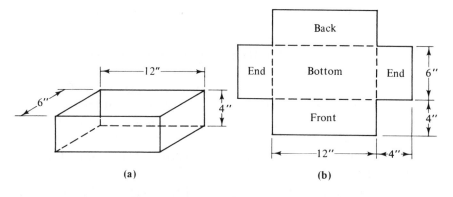

Figure 4-17 — A simple box layout.

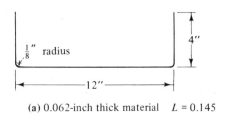

(a) 0.062-inch thick material $L = 0.145$

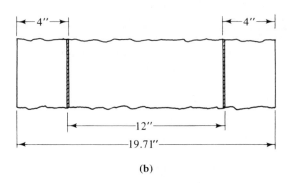

(b)

Figure 4-18 —— Section of a box pan.

Figure 4-18(b) shows the stretchout with shaded bend allowances. The first layout is the 4-inch side. To produce the 12-inch span of the section, two bends are used. Subtracting two bend allowances from the 12-inch side gives the layout of this section. Thus, $12 - 2(0.145) = 11.709$ inches in actual stretchout. It is a good practice to show the bend allowance areas defined by scribed lines. This then allows for the forming blades to align accurately for proper bending.

This stretchout was performed only on one section of the box's shape. To determine the stretchout of the other section, repeat the procedure given above. To determine stretchouts of the box form, follow the following steps.

1 / Compute the sum of the form (outside dimensions only) for both its length and width.
2 / Inspect to see that radius corners are of the same value. Count the total number used in each length and width section of the form.
3 / Using the metal thickness, temper, and inner radii, calculate the bend allowance L for one bend.
4 / Multiply this number by the total number of bends in each length and width section.
5 / Subtract the total from the summation of outside dimensions as performed in step 1.

[NOTE]

Length summation $=$ **A**
Width summation $=$ **B**. If five bends are used to form the length and three are used to form the width, the final stretch-out for each would be

$$\text{Length} = A - 5 \ (L)$$
$$\text{Width} = B - 3 \ (L)$$

where

$$L = \text{allowance for one bend}$$

[4-13]
a regular pyramid and its frustum

The layout of a pyramid or its frustum is most often limited to a four-sided figure. To define a frustum of a pyramid or cone, consider a cutting plane parallel to the base, such that it removes the upper section. The figure remaining below this cutting plane is called a frustum of the figure. However, regular pyramids with sides greater than four in number may be encountered. The following procedure showing a four-sided layout can be extended to any number of regular sides.

Figure 4-19 shows a typical drawing of a regular pyramid of four sides. The first operation when such a print is given is the determination of the figure's slant height(s). The slant height is the perpendicular distance from the figure's point or apex to a point on the base edge. This is shown in Fig. 4-19(a). The slant height in Fig. 4-19(b) is shown on the front view. The base length is of true length in both the top view and front view. With the slant height and base determined, a true-sized triangular face of the pyramid is constructed. Its construction is as follows. Produce a base edge line equal to that of the figure. By measurement, place a point at its midspan. Using a square butt and scale or geometric construction, draw a line perpendicular to the midpoint on the base line. Set dividers to a value equal to the slant height of the figure. With one end of the divider at the midpoint location of the base, scribe an arc so that it intersects the perpendicular. Draw straight lines from each end of the base to this point. This triangle is now a *true-sized triangle* of one of the pyramid's faces.

One may either make a sheet metal template cut to the shape of

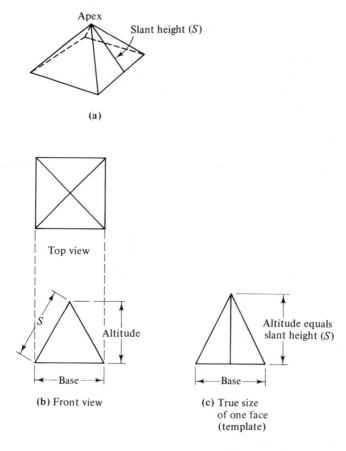

Figure 4-19 — Layout of a regular pyramid.

this triangle or construct the remaining faces as shown in Fig. 4-20, using construction principles of scale and divider. The method that is simpler and less error prone is the use of the template.

The basic form on the template is scribed on a flat sheet. This produces one face of the required pyramid. If the figure is four-sided, three additional adjacent forms are scribed with the apexes of each forming a common point. Bending along these lines will produce the required pyramid. The addition of a base cover is shown by dotted lines in the illustrated figure.

For developing a frustum of a pyramid, as shown in Fig. 4-21, the procedure is nearly identical to that for the regular pyramid. Construct a line equal to the length of the lower base. Find its midpoint and construct a line perpendicular to it with a value equal to the value

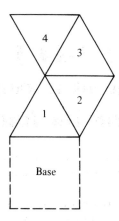

Figure 4-20 — Pattern of a regular pyramid of four sides.

of the slant height (s). Construct a line parallel to the lower base so that it passes through the upper limit of the perpendicular line. Set dividers to one-half the value of the upper base and scribe arcs about its midpoint. This defines the length of the upper base. Connect the ends of each base as shown in the figure. This, then, is the true shape of one side of the frustum. The procedures of layout as described for the regular pyramid can then be used.

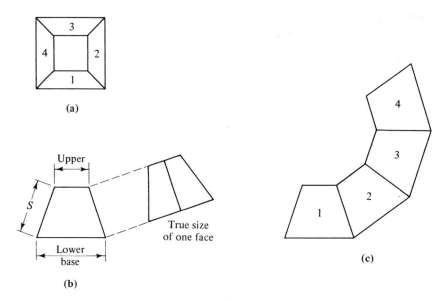

Figure 4-21 — Layout of a frustum of a regular pyramid.

[4-14]
layout of a regular
cone or its frustum

A regular cone or its frustum is an important shape often encountered in shop practice. The layout becomes a simple task if the logical steps given below are followed.

Figure 4-22(a) shows the basic shapes of the figure (regular cone or frustum). Figure 22(b) shows how the figure most often appears on a drawing or sketch. The information most basic to its layout is the diameter of the base circle and the slant height measurement(s).

The development of the stretchout for a given regular cone is as follows:

1 / Using the slant height distance as a radius, construct a circle.

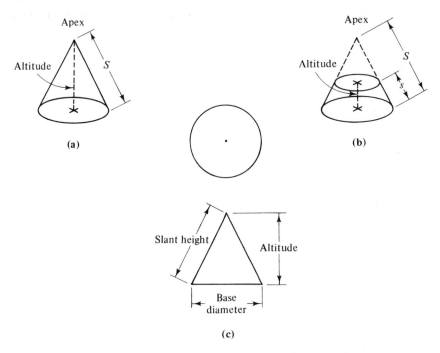

Figure 4-22 — Layout of a regular cone or a frustum of a cone.

2 / With the slant height distance as a radius, calculate the circumference of a full circle.

$$\text{Cir} = 2\pi s$$

where s = slant height dimension.

3 / Calculate the circumference of the base circle.

$$\text{Cir} = 2\pi r$$

where r = radius of base circle.

4 / Divide the circumference of the base circle by the circumference of the large circle.

5 / Multiply this value by 360 degrees.

6 / This value, called θ, is the angular portion of the large circle with radius *s* from which the cone is formed.

7 / Draw a radius line within the large circle.

8 / With a protractor aligned with the center of the circle and the radius line previously drawn, lay out the angular θ as calculated (steps 3, 4, and 5).

9 / Construct a second radius line from the center of the circle so that the angle θ is produced.

These basic steps to a regular cone layout are illustrated in Fig. 4-23.

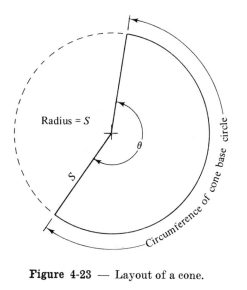

Figure 4-23 — Layout of a cone.

[4-15]
frustum of a cone

The layout of a frustum of a cone must always begin with the basic steps given for a regular cone. The formation of the upper circle is determined by using a radius whose value is $(S - s)$. This new radius is then produced on the layout, the original center point of the large circle, S, being used. This is shown in Fig. 4-24.

[4-16]
summary

Cones are formed by two basic methods: by forming on forming rolls or by bending along a series of equal spaced sectors. Typical sector lines for bending are shown as dotted radial lines in Fig. 4-24. The best approach to bend forming is to divide the angle θ into smaller values. These small angular values are then produced on the layout as small sectors. Small straight bends along these sector lines will approximate a true cone or frustum. Naturally, the greater number of sectors used, the more the cone will approach a true form.

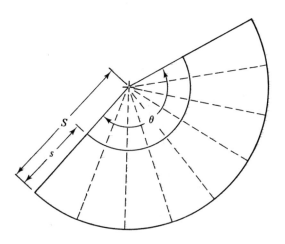

Figure 4-24 — Layout of a frustum of a cone.

For problems involving conic frustums, where the small base diameter is unknown or where the slant height S or small slant height are unknown, the following equations are offered.

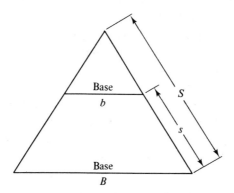

Figure 4-25

Given: B, b, s
Find: S

$$S = \frac{B \times s}{B - b} \qquad [4\text{--}6]$$

Given: S, B, s
Find: b

$$b = \frac{SB - Bs}{S} \qquad [4\text{--}7]$$

Given: S, B, b
Find: s

$$s = \frac{S(B - b)}{B} \qquad [4\text{--}8]$$

review questions

4-1 / What is the purpose of a drawing?

4-2 / Single view drawings are used under what conditions?

4-3 / In multi-view drawings, a part may have how many views? List these views. What is the name of this standard method of projections or views?

4-4 / What is the definition of a *dimensional tolerance?*

4-5 / In sheet metal, two tolerances are standard practice. List these tolerances in decimal values.

4-6 / When a metal section is deformed by bending, what two forces are introduced at the bend line?

4-7 / What is the purpose of calculating a bend allowance? What radius of bend is used—inner or outer?

4-8 / Calculate the bend allowance for 90° bends in 0.065 thick steel sheet for the following radii (use Equations [4-4] and [4-5]): (a) R = ½ inch; (b) R = ⁹⁄₃₂ inch; (c) R = ¹⁄₁₆ inch. Compare your answers with those in Table 4-2.

4-9 / When forming several or many workpieces of the same form, what should be a standard procedure to prove your calculations and operations?

4-10 / What dimensions are important in determining a stretchout from a print or sketch?

4-11 / Table 4-1 lists constants for equal spacings of 3 to 100 parts about a circle. Describe the basic approach used to prevent layout error.

4-12 / What is the main purpose of a template in sheet metal applications?

4-13 / In producing layouts for regular sided cones and pyramids or for frustums of cones and pyramids, what specific dimensions must be known before a layout begins?

4-14 / Calculations for bend allowances in pieces other than 90° require an operation called determining the *required angle.* Explain how this required angle is determined.

4-15 / What factors determine whether a K factor of 0.5 or 0.3 is used in the general bend equation?

5

bench tools for shearing and punching

[5-1]
introduction

Chapter 3 of this text presented what is considered to be a basic set of hand tools used within the sheet metal trade. These tools, however, are limited in both size and force to effectively operate on larger metal sections. This chapter is thus presented to both identify and describe those tools that are made available in the shop and are capable of larger work capacities in both the shearing and punching of heavy gauge sheet, plate, and rod products.

[5-2]
hand-operated shear

Hand-powered shears are designed to perform shearing and sizing operations on both prototype or short-run projects. These tools, with their hardened steel shear blades, are used on such materials as plastic, mica, leather, rubber, aluminum, copper, cold rolled steel, stainless steel, and leaded brass stock.

The size of a hand shear, Fig. 5-1, is specified by two factors: maximum shear width and material capacity, usually denoted as a gauge size (in mild steel). The normal range of hand shear sizes includes 6-inch, 12-inch, 24-inch, and 36-inch shears, all with a maximum gauge rating of 16 gauge (mild steel).

basic parts of the hand shear

The basic parts of the hand powered shear are the *main base,* containing the work surface and lower fixed shear blade, the *upper shear blade housing and blade,* and the *power train.*

The main base, usually of cast iron, contains a flat work surface for

Figure 5-1 — Hand operated shear. *(Courtesy of DI-ACRO/ Houdaille Industries Inc.)*

the work to rest on. Located at the back end of the work surface, a hardened and ground tool steel shear blade is located. The edge of the blade is level with the work surface. Two vertical steel columns rise from the base casting to provide a guide for the upper shear blade assembly.

Special attachments are available on most hand shears to aid the technician in working a particular project. These attachments include a graduated scale located to the right side of the work surface, an adjustable protractor gauge, and, most important, a quick-set micrometer spacing gauge located at the rear end of the lower housing.

The graduated scale on the work platen serves two purposes. The edge of the scale is factory set so that it is at an angle of 90 degrees to the shear blades. This edge or scale is used when pieces must be sheared with adjoining sides having a 90-degree angle. Thus, square or rectangular pieces make use of this reference edge. The graduations on this scale are set so that any specific reading is referenced to the edge of the shear. This scale should be used for sizes only within a tolerance range of $\pm\frac{1}{64}$ inch. When shear sizes must be of closer tolerance, the micrometer depth bar is used. Two threaded rods extend from the back end of the shear base. Located on each of these two threaded rods is a micrometer nut generally graduated in 0.001-inch increments. A gauge bar spans the width and terminates at the bottom of each of the micrometer adjust nuts. Most of these micrometer adjust gauges are designed so that inward pressure toward the screw thread will allow the adjusting nuts to be moved rapidly to new or various locations along their threaded rods. This arrangement allows accurately sized shear pieces to be produced on both small and large runs.

The normal procedure used in setting up a close tolerance size with the micrometer gauge is as follows. Adjust the gauge bar approximately to size with a steel scale. This is performed by placing the end of the scale against the back shear face of the lower blade and measuring the required dimension to the face of the gauge bar. This is done at both ends of the shear bar depth gauge to approximate a parallel condition. The final operation involves making several test shears on a thin strip of metal. The first test shear is performed at the right side of the shear. After shearing, the test piece is sized for correctness. The amount of "over" or "under" size is then corrected by using the micrometer adjust nut on the right side. The second test shear is used on the left side micrometer. Again an "over" or "under" size reading is corrected with the left side micrometer. As a final check, return to the right side micrometer and shear a third test piece. This is done to verify correctness of size. When the gauge bar is positioned properly, lock the two micrometer nuts with their built-in locking screws so that accidental movement of the gauged bar is eliminated. Since each micrometer nut is independent in adjustment, the gauge bar can be set at specific angles with respect to the shear blades. Thus, if a rectangular flat sheet is to be sheared with one edge out of parallel with its parent edge, the gauge bar can be set so as to produce this offset.

The protractor gauge, located generally at the left side of the work platen, is provided for producing such cuts as 45-, 30-, or 60-degree or other specific angles. This gauge is triangular in shape and is secured to the work surface by three holding screws located in slots machined into the gauge.

Using a bevel protractor and scale, one can obtain accurate angles with respect to the shear blades. The general procedure for setting the protractor gauge is as follows. Set the required angle on a protractor and scale; lock the setting. Place the protractor edge at one outer edge of the work platen. Adjust the gauge until alignment with the scale is achieved. Lock the gauge.

upper shear blade housing

The upper housing of the hand shear is the movable section of this tool. Motion is confined to an up and down action, which is defined by two vertical guides affixed to the shear base. The upper shear blade is contained within the framework of this housing and is set so that in a downward motion, the upper shear blade and the lower shear blade pass one another with a zero or near zero clearance. This closeness of the shear edges, coupled with the fact that the top blade is set slightly out of parallel with the bottom blade, provides a smooth effortless shearing of the material (Fig. 5-2).

hand shear power train

The up and down motion of the shear blade assembly is produced by a handle-cam combination.

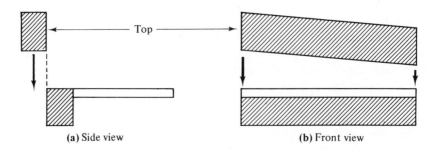

(a) Side view   (b) Front view

Figure 5-2 — Shear blade arrangement.

Located at each end of the upper housing is a cam or off-center casting. This cam casting is attached to each end of the upper housing and a common eccentric shaft containing the handle. Pushing the handle toward the back of the shear causes the cams to raise the upper shear blade so that work may be positioned. Pulling the handle toward the front of the shear causes the upper shear blade to lower slowly with tremendous power to shear the material within its blade area.

work holddowns

During any shearing operation, such as that described above, two distinct effects are produced on the material being sheared. The first effect, particularly with dull shear blades, is the tendency for the material to back away from the cutting edges. The second effect, sometimes called *kick,* is the raising of the material off the work platen as the blades begin their shearing action.

On many shears, particularly those with large width and gauge capacity, a series of metal fingers or holddowns are provided. These holddowns are located along the entire length of the upper blade housing and in most cases are spring-loaded. The function of these holddown fingers is to clamp the material flat to the work platen and prevent both *backout* and *kick* during shearing. When shearing soft materials such as copper or aluminum, one must be careful that excess pressure from the holddowns does not produce depressions or dents in the material.

shear blades

The two shear blades of any shear are made of hardened and ground tool steel. In some instances, where hard material requires, blades of high chrome content are available for long wear.

The blades are generally made with a rectangular cross section and are ground flat and square on all four sides. Mounting holes are located along the wide faces of the blades for both mounting and removal.

When the blades become dull, they may be removed and rotated in order to use any of the three remaining sharp edges. On rare occasions, the blades must be removed and reground on a surface grinder to rejuvenate the cutting edges. This grinding most often is done on the narrow faces of the shear blade. Should grinding be performed on the long side faces of the blades to remove burrs or nicks, the blades must be shimmed or spaced on remounting.

Suppose that in resharpening a set of shear blades, the machinist had to reduce the thickness of the blades a total of 0.025 inch to remove nicks or burrs. If one then simply installed the blades, it would be found that the top and bottom blade had a gap of 0.025 inch. This large gap would prove very ineffective in shearing and would bend and tear the material instead of shearing it.

To compensate for the diminished blade thickness, a brass or steel shim must be placed between the bottom blade and its mating surface. If a clearance between the two blades is to be approximately 0.001 inch, a shim of 0.024 inch would be used. This would space the lower blade toward the upper blade and leave a clearance of 0.001 inch. After the blades have been checked for clearance, the back up screws are used to adjust and support the blades during shearing operations.

The top surface of the bottom blade is adjusted so that its face is level with the work platen.

Remember to offset the top blade slightly out of parallel with the bottom blade to produce the ''shear'' line. Figure 5-3 illustrates this arrangement.

[5-3]
power shears

For shearing large-width sheet and plate products, power shears are produced. Power shears can be foot-powered or motor-powered as the larger types are. A typical small-sized power shear is seen in Fig. 5-4.

Power shears are generally obtainable in three sizes—the 24⅛-inch, 37¾-inch and 50-inch. In most cases, these shears are limited to 16-gauge mild steel or thinner. Gauge bars are available in both the front and back of the machine. The gauge bar in the rear is, in many cases, of the mi-

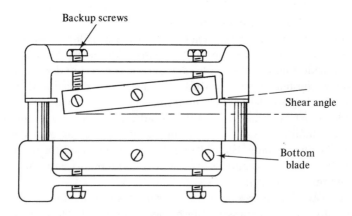

Figure 5-3

Figure 5-4 — Power shear. *(Courtesy of DI-ACRO/Houdaille Industries Inc.)*

crometer type with 0.001-inch increments and 0.100 inch for a full revolution. The front gauge bar is very useful when the need to shear narrow widths from previously sheared forms is necessary.

A side squaring gauge bar is located at the right side of the work platen. This is the gauge used to produce 90-degree shear cuts on a workpiece. A protractor gauge is also available to perform shear cuts other than those of a 90-degree nature. Work holddowns are supplied with all power shears.

Power for the shear, other than the foot or kick shear, is supplied by an electric motor of high torque/high slip. A clutching and flywheel arrangement allows the blades to shear at any speed within the machine's range for single strokes, or it can be set up to operate at strokes up to 100 per minute or higher. The automatic strokes allow the technician to continuously feed stock into the shear and thus perform what is termed high-volume or production-sheared parts. Power is controlled by either a foot pedal or a hand lever that operates the clutch.

In the single-stroke mode, the pedal or hand lever can be jogged so that the shear blades will operate at slower speeds. For automatic cycling, the pedal or lever can be fully engaged so that the up and down strokes of the shear will repeat at their determined cycle.

Larger power shears are used to shear plate up to $\frac{1}{4}$ inch in steel or $\frac{1}{2}$ inch in aluminum plate. Width capacity of these larger types is up to 10 feet. With these larger capacity shears, plate sizes can normally be sheared within length and width dimensions of $\pm\frac{1}{8}$ inch or less.

The foot- or "kick"-powered shear is so named because a sharp downward force causes the shear to operate. The kick or foot bar is located near the floor of the machine housing and is connected to the upper shear bar through rod linkage. After a cut, release of the foot pressure raises the shear blade for the next stroke.

[5-4]
care of shears

The cardinal rule in protecting a shear from permanent damage is never to shear material thicker than that recommended by the manufacturer. Failure to follow this rule could cause the housing to warp or crack.

Blades should be inspected regularly for dulling or nicking. Regrind or rotate to a new edge as previously described. Inspect to make sure that blade clamping and backup screws are secure.

Lubricate, according to the manufacturer's instructions, those points of a sliding or rotating nature. Should a shear be inactive for a length of time, coat the blades with a protective film of oil to prevent rust.

One final note: whenever blades on a powered shear are being reset or removed, be sure that the power is switched off and that a tag is placed at the power switch stating why it is off. This will prevent accidental turnon and possible serious injury to the person working on the machine.

This first portion of the chapter has introduced many of the shears that the technician will encounter. Understanding of their basic design and function is essential to build the confidence needed when one is operating this most important tool. A sampling of some of the typical shapes that can be produced with the shear are shown in Fig. 5-5.

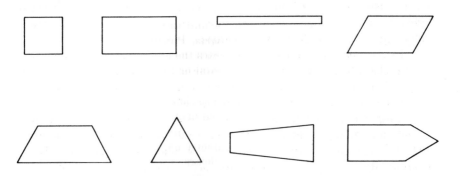

Figure 5-5 — Typical sheared shapes.

[5-5]
bench notchers

Sheet metal notchers are tools that serve two specific purposes in the metal trades, producing notches and producing tab cuts. These operations are important in the formation of metal boxes or chassis.

Before we discuss the basics of this machine, let us define the terms *notch* and *tab*. Let us consider a square sheet of metal of dimensions 6 inches by 6 inches (Fig. 5-6).

This stretchout is to be formed into a box having dimensions of 4 inches by 4 inches with 1-inch-high sides. For this example, let us assume that no bend allowance is made. To prepare the sheet so that the sides can be formed at angles of 90 degrees to the base, corner *notches* must be

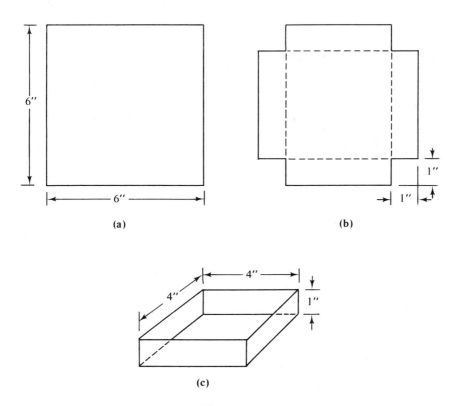

(a)　　　　　　　　　　　　　(b)

(c)

Figure 5-6

placed at each corner [Fig. 5-6(b)]. These corner cutouts in our example are 1 inch by 1 inch. Thus, bending along the dotted bend lines, we form the sides of our box tray [Fig. 5-6(c)]. To retain the shape of this box tray, the corners may be welded, soldered, or fastened in some other fashion. Should our box have had a bend radius and thickness given, the depth of the notch would have to be calculated by using the bend allowance formulas given previously.

For our illustration of what a tab is, let us look at the box tray shown in Fig. 5-7. This box is of the same basic dimensions as that in Fig. 5-6, but with one added feature. Two opposite sides of the box have extensions on either end that are bent at angles of 90 degrees to the side and lie along the faces of the remaining two box sides. These extensions are called *tabs*. Tabs in chassis provide two important functions: They add strength and rigidity to the box, and they provide a convenient arrangement such that bolts, rivets, or sheet metal screws may be used to maintain the final shape. Again as in our previous example, no bend allowances are included. In actual practice, however, both the notch and tab dimensions must be set by using the allowance formulas given previously.

basics of the notcher

Let us now look at the actual tool used to produce these special cutouts called notches and tab notches.

The hand-operated notcher shown in Fig. 5-8 is somewhat similar to the standard shear in operation. The work platen or base contains two hardened tool steel blades that are set at an angle of 90 degrees to each other. Located above the platen and attached to a movable ram is the

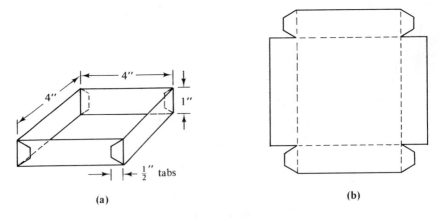

(a)

(b)

Figure 5-7 — Box tray.

Figure 5-8 — Hand operated notcher. *(Courtesy of DI-ACRO/ Houdaille Industries Inc.)*

upper shear blade assembly, also containing two shear blades at an angle of 90 degrees to each other. The upper and lower blades are set into machined pockets that allow the shear blades to pass in close contact when the action of the notcher is actuated. The size of a notcher is determined by two parameters: the length of the 90-degree cut achieved by the blades, and its material gauge limit. The most common size of hand notcher is the 6-inch, 16-gauge type. This description merely states that it will shear a 6-inch by 6-inch 90-degree notch in material up to and including 16-gauge mild steel sheet.

Should smaller-sized notches or notches of a rectangular fashion be required, they may be accurately gauged on the work platen.

Two depth gauge stops are located on the work surface. These depth gauges are adjustable independently and are positioned at an angle of 90 degrees with respect to each other.

Generally, a graduated scale affixed to the platen will indicate the distance at which the stop is set, as measured from the corner point of the shear blade's arrangement. Thus, if a notch with dimensions of 1¾ inches by 1¾ inches were required, each stop would be adjusted so that it would read a distance of 1¾ inches as indicated by the scale or as measured from the corner of the bottom shear blades. The two stops are locked at their positions with screw hardware of either a hex head or allen socket type. Should a rectangular notch be required, one that has 90-degree sides of different lengths, the stops can be so set to produce the notch.

notches greater than 90 degrees

Notches greater than 90 degrees can be produced with a hand notcher by the following method. Let us consider a notch of 120 degrees that is to be produced. For this example, let us consider that the notch has sides of equal length (Fig. 5-9).

As can be seen, the initial line of the 120-degree angle, line *A*, can be formed in the first notch operation. Remember that the notcher will produce only 90-degree notches at any one operation; thus, a second shear operation must be performed to achieve the final angle. By simple subtraction, 120 − 90 = 30 degrees; the final line of the 120-degree angle, line *B*, is determined by a second shearing operation. This final notch operation is in most cases achieved by aligning the "laid out" angle to shear edges of the notcher. In multiple operations, however, the stops on the work platen can be set to define one of the angle's sides. The second side can then be set by using a scratch line layout and setting the platen stops so that the shear blades align on the last line of the required notch.

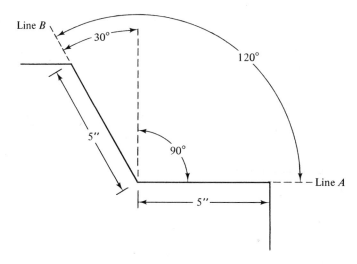

Figure 5-9 — A notch greater than 90°.

tabs

The operation of producing tabs is performed both accurately and speedily by modifying the basic shear blades of the notcher. This operation, however, requires the adjustment of both top and bottom blade pairs. To better understand this process, let us refer to Fig. 5-10.

Figure 5-10(a) shows an initial notch operation performed on a flat sheet. The dotted-line section, called a *tab,* must now be produced. On the hand-operated notcher equipped with independent blades the following operation is performed. Loosen the bottom blades so that they may be independently adjusted along their mitered (45-degree) joint (Fig. 5-11).

Motion by either blade 1 or 2 or a combination of both is adjusted

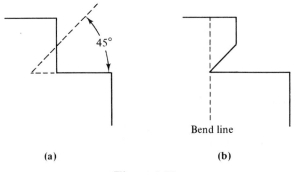

Figure 5-10

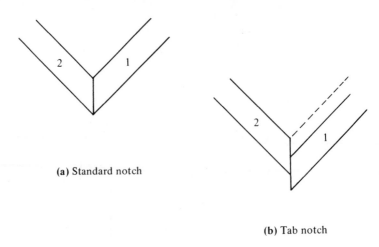

(a) Standard notch

(b) Tab notch

Figure 5-11

to produce the required tab notch size. On machines of 6- by 6-inch size, the maxium size tab that can be produced is a 1- by 1-inch size. Remember that this tab is, in actuality, a 45-degree cutout. Secure the fastening screws on the adjusted bottom blades. With the top blade loosened, lower the assembly slowly until the upper blades come in contact with the lower fixed and positioned blades. Move the upper blades in or out until they meet the shear edges of their mating lower blades. Secure the upper blades in their mated position in respect to the lower blade configuration. The required tab is now set. The position or stop plates can now be set and locked to produce the required tab on one piece or on a multipiece job.

As described above, the hand-operated notcher-tab tool is a versatile and important tool in the metal trade. This tool in most cases is powered by a hand lever located at the top of the main casting. Pulling down produces a downward work stroke, while pushing toward the back of the tool retracts the shear blades from the workpiece.

Power notchers and tab cutters are available which operate from a floor pedal control. In the continuous operation mode, strokes of up to 180 per minute can be obtained where high production runs of the same part are required.

Care of these tools generally falls into two areas, maintaining sharp shearing edges and proper and frequent lubrication of moving parts with lubricants specified by the manufacturer. In long operations on parts having the same operations, frequent checks of shear blade fasteners and stock stops should be made.

[5-6]
rod parters

The need to cut rods of various diameters to specific lengths is an often encountered shop operation. One may use either a hacksaw or a hand saw to perform this operation, but a faster and more accurate method is found in the rod parter (Fig. 5-12).

The hand-powered rod parter is a tool designed to shear solid rods of various sizes and materials to specific lengths. These tools are specified by the diameter of the largest rod that they will part. Generally, there are two sizes, a $\frac{3}{8}$-inch parter and a $\frac{5}{8}$-inch parter. The $\frac{3}{8}$-inch capacity parter has 11 holes, which range from $\frac{1}{16}$ inch through and including a $\frac{3}{8}$-inch hole. Hole graduations vary by $\frac{1}{32}$-inch increments. The $\frac{5}{8}$-inch parter normally has 10 holes that range from $\frac{1}{16}$ inch through and including a $\frac{5}{8}$-inch hole. Hole size graduations in parters of this size nor-

Figure 5-12 — Rod parter. (*Courtesy of DI-ACRO/Houdaille Industries Inc.*)

mally vary by $\frac{1}{16}$-inch increments. Shearing heads are also available for parting square, rectangular, and hexagonal solid bar stock. The parting action is performed by two shear plates. The stationary or fixed plate is that in which the material is inserted. The shearing plate, the second plate, is affixed to a cam-actuated hand-powered handle. Pulling the handle causes the shearing plate to rotate in relation to the stationary plate. This action is then responsible for the parting of a rod placed within the selected hole.

To the right side of the rod parter, a rod with an adjustable stop plate is provided. The stop plate is secured to the rod with a clamping screw. This arrangement allows for specific lengths to be set between the shear line and stop plate. After the stop plate is locked, multiple rod cutting of the same length can be performed by merely inserting the rod to the fixed stop and parting.

rod parter blades

The shear blade heads on a parter are normally made for two specific types of rods: cold rolled and hot rolled. The type of product used has a direct bearing on the shear plate hole clearance. When only cold rolled products are used, the holes are made approximately 0.003 inch oversize. Hot rolled products, however, are not as uniform in their dimensions, and the holes are made approximately 0.015 inch oversize. It is quite possible that an attempt to part hot rolled rod will meet with difficulty if shears specified for cold formed products are used. This problem is, as stated above, due to the rod diameter's exceeding the clearance in the shear hole. The rod can be inserted into the next larger hole and sheared, but a burred and somewhat distorted shear end on the rod will result.

The two circular shear heads are mounted in their respective housings by means of screw fasteners. These heads, made of hardened tool steel, are ground with parallel faces, which offer an added work-life feature. Should the parting action show signs of burring or mashing, either of the shear heads may be removed and turned so as to expose a new shear surface. What this means is that there are four surfaces, two on each shear head, that can be used before the heads must be resharpened.

Rod parters as detailed in the above discussion are designed to shear *solid* sections of round, square, rectangular, or hexagonal rod. Shearing tubing or pipe should never be attempted by this tool, since the action will merely crush and jam the workpiece in the shear head section.

Power rod parters are available, and their chief purpose is to produce large runs of rods at high rates per minute. With an electric motor-flywheel combination, parting cycles up to 180 per minute and more are obtainable.

Care of these tools, again like that of the hand shear, falls into two areas. The shear heads should be inspected for burr-free partings. Should burring become a problem, rotate one of the heads to expose a new shear face edge. Lubricate moving parts of the tool according to use and factory recommendations. During periods of inactivity, wipe the shear heads with oil to prevent rusting. After parting operations on hot rolled products, remove the flakes of scale that have gotten into moving or sliding surfaces. This scale is abrasive in nature and if not removed could cause wear to take place in critical areas of the tool.

One final note: when working on the die heads of power rod parters, be sure to unplug and tag the machine power cord. This will prevent accidental operation and possible injury to fingers and hands within the shear head area.

[5-7]
punching tools—
introduction

Most, if not all, sheet metal forms start in what is called a stretchout or flatout state. This merely means that the physical dimensions, shapes, and holes of a workpiece are produced on the flatout material prior to the final forming or shaping of the workpiece.

We have, to this point, discussed several of the various tools used to produce the basic form and size of a product. These tools are the shear, the notcher, and the rod parter.

The second phase in preparing the workpiece before forming is the placement of holes. The holes can be round, square, rectangular, hexagonal, or some other geometric form. These holes may be required for fasteners, meters, buttons, valves, lights, or any number of other items that will be mounted on the finished product.

In the sheet metal trade, the most often used method of producing holes is by use of a punch and die. See Fig. 5-13. In effect, a punch and die must be used in combination. The punch, called the *male*, is made in the desired cross-sectional shape and dimension of a specific hole. The die, called the *female*, contains the same cross-sectional shape of the punch, but with a slightly larger size called the *die clearance*. This clearance between the punch and die is essential to perform a "punching"

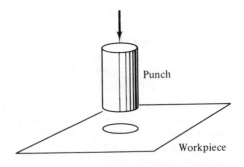

Punch

Workpiece

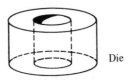

Die

Figure 5-13

operation with minimum wear on the two dies and also effectively pierce a piece of material located between the two. Punching is thus defined as the process of producing a hole of some specified shape in a workpiece by the shearing action of a punch and die. This action is not a cutting action, but a punching or shearing operation. Pressure applied to the punch forces against a workpiece and die, with the result being a shearing of the metal in a shape defined by the punch and die.

[5-8]
the punch press

The punch press is a tool designed for two main functions: to hold in alignment a punch and die and to supply a directed force by hand or power to the punch such that it punches or shears through material located between the lower mating die. A typical hand punch press is shown in Fig. 5-14.

The punch press is rated in several ways as to its performance: depth of throat, work capacity, and material capacity.

Figure 5-14 — Hand punch press. *(Courtesy of DI-ACRO/ Houdaille Industries Inc.)*

The depth of throat rating is merely a size designation stating the distance that exists between the punch and die center and the back of the supporting frame. For example, in using a 6-inch punch, that one may punch to the center of a 12-inch diameter piece of work or punch to within 6 inches of the side of a rectangular or square workpiece.

The work capacity of a press is rated in tons of force that are available through either hand or power operation.

The third item, material capacity, is most often defined as the maximum diameter hole that can be punched in a particular gauge of mild steel. Most hand punch presses are capable of punching a 4-inch diameter hole in 16-gauge mild steel. Heavier material is usually punched by using the powered presses.

basics of the punch press

The main frame of the punch press is of either a cast or fabricated construction. At the top portion of the press, a cam- or gear-operated lever delivers an upward or downward force to the ram located within the ram guide housing. The ram or turret is thus the movable part of the press which holds the punch of the punch and die set. In most presses of the hand type, the ram contains a 1-inch diameter hole in its end to accept the shank of the punch. A screw often is used to secure the punch.

Located below the ram is the work platen into which the die is located and secured. The size of the die hole varies in all presses and can be specified as an A, B, C, D, or E. The diameters of these letter-designated dies are $1\frac{1}{4}$, $2\frac{1}{8}$, $2\frac{3}{4}$, $3\frac{3}{4}$, and $4\frac{3}{4}$ inches.

Attached to the turret of the punch press is a device called a *stripper*. The stripper's main function is to initially bear and clamp the workpiece as the punch makes contact. After punching, the stripper maintains a spring pressure force on the material as the punch retracts. The action is called stripping the material from the punch. The two metal holddown arms attached to the stripper are adjustable and are spring loaded for various thicknesses of material.

alignment of punch and die

Installation of a punch and die into a press is a relatively easy operation. The first operation is to examine both punch and die to see that they are of the required size and shape. It is also good practice to inspect for chips or cracks that may have developed in these tools. Replace or have them reground by a machine shop. Install and lock the die into its recessed holder. Secure it with screw pressure applied to the ground flat on the periphery. Install the shank of the punch into the ram and lightly secure with its locking screw. The punch should be able to rotate slightly with hand pressure. Should the punch and die be of a shape other than a round, perform the following alignment step. Slowly bring the punch to the face of the die. Rotate the punch until it penetrates into the die. Hold this position and secure firmly the punch in the ram. Repeat the cycle slowly again to insure alignment of the punch and die. The final operation is the adjustment of the stripper. The best method of performing this operation is to take a test or scrap piece of material and proceed to punch a hole. As the ram is retracted, the stripper should slide the metal piece from the punch.

One final note should be made before we move to our next discussion. Most, if not all, punches whose shapes are round, square, hexagonal, or some other regular geometric form have a ground conical point on the end face of the punch. The purpose of this center point is so that one may locate it in center-punched hole locations on a flat sheet. This is useful when one-of-a-kind pieces must be punched with no great location accuracy.

punch gauge stops

When it is required accurately to locate and punch holes in many pieces of the same form, the punch gauges are used. These gauges are located at an angle of 90 degrees to each other at the back and right side of the work table. The more simple and less accurate form is merely a stop plate that is positioned and locked to a rod. Thus, if both front and back stops are positioned to the center line of the punch, holes can be located and punched repeatedly. Some presses are equipped with vernier screw dials. These graduated dials will move their stops 0.100 inch per revolution. Incremented about the dial are smaller graduations that allow for movements in position of 0.001 inch.

[5-9]
multipunch
turret press

A versatile tool used in model and short-run production shops is the multistation turret punch press (Fig. 5-15).

Most common are the 12- and 18-station turrets. This form of press can be set up to contain many of the commonly used punch and die sizes in round holes. Often the 12-position turret is set up with punches and dies from $\frac{1}{8}$ inch through $1\frac{1}{2}$ inches in diameter, while the 16-position turret is set up through the same range but includes diameters not found in the 12-station turret. The real convenience and speed of this tool can be seen in a punching operation where there are many holes of various sizes. The top and the bottom turret of a required size are simply rotated under the ram, and that punch is ready to be used.

Turrets may be operated in two fashions: independent rotation and locking of the upper and lower turret or, in some cases, simultaneous rotation via a geared hand wheel. Both the upper punch turret and lower die turret are marked so that mismatching of the dies is not a problem.

In the case where the lower turret must be hand-rotated, locate it by using the station number. Lock the turrets from rotating with the aligning handle located near the rear of the machine frame.

Strippers are built into each station of the top turret. This means that any punch being used will use only the stripper associated with that punch.

Figure 5-15 — Multistation turret punch press. *(Courtesy of DI-ACRO/Houdaille Industries Inc.)*

Many, if not all, of the turret punch presses that you will encounter will contain vernier travel dials to accurately set punch locations on your workpiece. Their operation is the same as previously described for the hand punch press.

When punch or turret punch presses are used, be sure that all hardware securing punches or dies is properly fastened. Moving parts should be oiled or greased according to the manufacturer's recommendation.

In turret punch setups, it is common practice to have a chart prepared stating what size each station will punch. Should you need to change such a setup, it is most important that you replace the dies so that sizes will agree with the chart. This is important so that the next person using this tool does not punch a hole of the wrong size due to your changing the setup.

If, during punching of thin sheet, burrs begin to appear around the hole, check first for punch-to-die alignment. If after alignment the burring still exists, it is a good chance that the punch and die need to be resharpened. Never attempt to punch material thicker than that specified by the limits of the machine.

Finally, after any metal punching or removal operation, be sure to remove the blankings and chips from the machine, particularly in areas such as work surfaces, adjustment screws, etc. In general, clean the machine and leave it so that the next person can begin his operations without first cleaning what you have left behind.

[5-10]
small hand and
chassis punches

Situations often arise where the shape of a part or finished chassis must be changed by the addition of new holes. This situation is most often corrected with some basic hand tools using hand squeezing power or torque applied by a wrench to a hand die punch.

the hand-held punch

The hand-held punch, shown in Fig. 5-16, is a most useful tool, and in some cases the technician may want to acquire one as his personal tool.

The hand punch is a tool developed to punch holes up to $\frac{1}{4}$ inch in diameter in 16-gauge mild steel.

The basic tool is designed to accept a wide range of punches and dies. This range most often includes $\frac{3}{32}$-, $\frac{1}{8}$-, $\frac{5}{32}$-, $\frac{3}{16}$-, $\frac{7}{32}$-, $\frac{1}{4}$-, and $\frac{9}{32}$-inch diameters.

The main lower assembly contains the working throat of the punch and also holds the die in alignment.

The throat depth is, on the smaller hand punches, approximately $1\frac{3}{4}$ inches. Larger punches with capacities up to $\frac{1}{2}$ inch in diameter have throat depths to $2\frac{1}{4}$ inches.

On many models, an adjustable graduated gauge is supplied. Thus, punching holes at specific distances from the edge of a sheet may be done with repeated accuracy.

The dies in general are externally threaded. This allows for them to be installed, adjusted, or removed by simply turning the die in or out of the tapped hole. The punch, however, is guided by the hole in the top of the throat casting. Power for the punch is produced in the upper

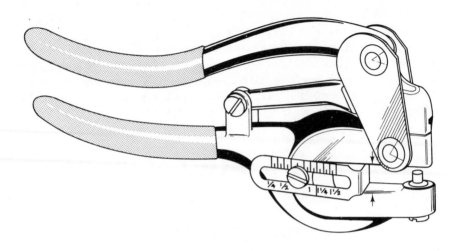

Figure 5-16 — Hand punch.

handle of the tool. The upper handle uses a cam effect on the punch holder assembly located between the two handles. The effect is translated to an up and down motion of the punch holder and punch.

To remove a punch, the following procedure is recommended. Loosen the small knurled screw holding the punch holder assembly to the lower handle. Raise the upper handle and pull the now loosened end of the punch holder back until the punch is free of the "T" slot. Remove the punch and replace it with the next required size punch. Push the free end of the punch holder assembly until it captures the end of the punch. Align the mounting hole and insert and secure the knurled fastening screw.

Whenever punch and die changes are made, always be sure that the pair is "mated" (same size and type).

Before using this type of tool, center punch the center of all the holes to be punched on your workpiece. This allows for accurate alignment of the punch, as the conical point on its face is for just that purpose.

Larger hand punches are available with a full range from $\frac{1}{16}$-inch to $\frac{1}{2}$-inch diameters. These sizes are incremented by $\frac{1}{64}$ inch.

the chassis punch

A simple but often used hand tool in the sheet metal trades is the chassis punch. This relatively inexpensive punch and die is manufactured in a wide range of sizes and shapes. Round, square, rectangular, and triangular holes, and special shapes unique to the electronics field are readily available.

The true value of this tool can be seen in the fact that special shapes can be blanked in material up to 16-gauge mild steel. Power for this tool is in most cases obtained by drawing the two halves of the punch together with the turning of a screw. In some cases, hydraulic pressure from a portable unit can be used to draw the punch assembly together.

The chassis punch is best at what is called "field modification." This is defined as performing some operation on an assembly at its working location, as removal back to the shop would prove costly or inappropriate.

details and operation of the chassis punch

The typical chassis punch consists of the basic parts: punch, die, draw bolt, and nut. This assembly is shown in Fig. 5-17.

The punch, as is the die, is made of hardened and ground tool steel. It contains a hole through its axis. The die section is designed for two functions. It contains the shaped pocket of the punch form and, on its opposite face, a recess for the rectangular-headed draw bolt.

To explain the use and operation of this tool, let us begin with the initial preparation of the material to be punched. The shape of the hole, be it round, square, or some other shape, should first be laid out. This is particularly important when square holes are produced, so that the sides are oriented properly to some edge or function.

Next, locate the geometric center of the shape on the layout. Using either the chassis punch bolt size or the factory recommendation, produce a drilled hole on the center to just allow the body of the draw bolt to pass through it.

Figure 5-17 — Basics of a chassis punch. (*Courtesy of Greenlee Tool Co.*)

If possible, clamp the head of the draw bolt in a vise and place the die over the bolt, shear edge up. Next place the material with its pre-drilled hole over the bolt with its layout side up. Place the punch over the bolt body and install the nut over the exposed threaded end. Note that the working end of all chassis punches has curved and beveled cutting edges. This is an important design factor, since it allows the punch to enter and slice the material with greater ease than if its work end were flat. By applying force to the nut with a wrench, the punch is forced through the material to the die located beneath the workpiece. The application of a coat of oil or grease to the punch, die, and threads of the draw bolt will ease the operation considerably.

After the operation is completed, remove the draw nut, punch, and workpiece. The punched blank is now located at the bottom of the die. This should be removed before the next operation or before the tool is stored.

In odd-shaped chassis punches, a method of using keys in the punch and die is used to maintain the punch and die alignment. See Fig. 5-18.

review questions

5-1 / What is the general size range of hand operated shears?

5-2 / List the main parts of the hand shear.

5-3 / Describe the special attachments found on the hand shear.

5-4 / During a shear operation what two effects are imposed on the sheet metal? How can these effects be minimized?

Figure 5-18 — Keyed chassis punch. *(Courtesy of Greenlee Tool Co.)*

5-5 / Why is the top shear blade at a slight angle to the fixed bottom blade?

5-6 / Bench notchers are sized by two important capacities; what are they?

5-7 / Define a *notch* and a *tab*.

5-8 / What is the notch angle range for the bench notcher?

5-9 / How is the workpiece positioned on the table of the notcher so that multiple piece runs will be identical?

5-10 / To produce a notch of 145°, describe the technique employed to produce this required notch.

5-11 / How are rod parters sized?

5-12 / While parting a large run of a certain diameter rod, you notice that you must put increasingly more power into the parter and that the sheared rod ends are ragged and burred. What would you do to eliminate these problems?

5-13 / Power shears are often employed where large runs must be made. What is the maximum number of parting cycles that can be obtained with this type of machine?

5-14 / What is the purpose of a punch and die?

5-15 / Punch presses are rated in three areas; list them.

5-16 / Die holes in punch presses are often sized in letters. List these letters and their corresponding hole diameters.

5-17 / What is the purpose of a stripper on a punch press?

5-18 / Two general types of punch presses are found in most shops. What are they called?

5-19 / Using the micrometer dials of a punch press, what accuracy can be achieved?

5-20 / List some indications that a punch and die is becoming dull.

5-21 / Hand held punches are invaluable for field work. What are the general hole sizes and the gauge materials that they will punch?

5-22 / What is the main purpose of a chassis punch?

5-23 / What means of power is most often used in chassis punch operations?

6

bench tools for forming

[6-1]
introduction

Forming operations in sheet metal can be listed as three main types: straight bends, cylindrical bends, and curved bends. These three types or their combinations make up most, if not all, of the many sheet metal parts and forms in use today. This chapter will discuss four main bench tools used to produce these shapes; they are the leaf brake, the press brake, slip rollers, and tube bar benders.

[6-2]
the leaf brake—
purpose and size

A hand-operated tool designed to produce straight bends in metal through a wide range of angles is the leaf-box brake, Fig. 6-1. This metal working tool is mostly limited to working 16-gauge mild steel in various lengths, with the maximum length determined by the length of the bending bars. The sizes of hand brakes are thus specified by the maximum sheet width that will enter the working area. The more common sizes are the 6-, 12-, 24-, and 36-inch brakes. Before discussing the makeup, use, and applications of the leaf brake, let us discuss some of the more common straight bends performed with this tool.

straight bend forms

The leaf brake is capable of producing a variety of bends to meet most fabrication and form requirements. The most common bend, however, is the 90-degree bend. This is used in forming square or rectangular boxes.

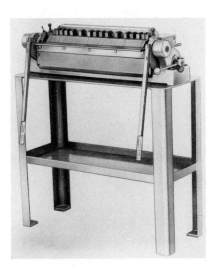

Figure 6-1 — Leaf-box brake. *(Courtesy of DI-ACRO/Houdaille Industries Inc.)*

Angles greater or less than 90 degrees can be produced with the leaf brake.

Angles greater than 90 degrees are called *obtuse angles,* and those less than 90 degrees are called *oblique angles.* The above bends as well as some of the more common other forms of bends are illustrated in Fig. 6-2.

Each of the bend sections, whether in combination or in modified form, make up most of the straight bends that are in common use. In bend sections such as the *flange, offset,* and *reverse* there are limitations as to the height of a section that can be produced on a leaf brake. These limitations will be discussed shortly.

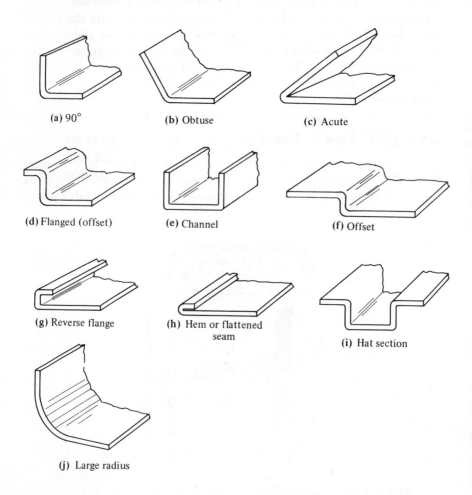

(a) 90° (b) Obtuse (c) Acute

(d) Flanged (offset) (e) Channel (f) Offset

(g) Reverse flange (h) Hem or flattened seam (i) Hat section

(j) Large radius

Figure 6-2 — Bends.

basics of the leaf brake

The basic parts of a leaf brake are main housing, forming bar, forming bar adjustment, front leaf assembly, and clamping and adjustable back gauge stops.

The *main housing* of the brake is generally produced in cast iron or steel for both strength and durability. Located between the ends of the housing is a flat fixed metal work surface, while above this surface is a hardened and ground forming bar. The *forming bar* is attached to a cam-operated lever so that it can be raised or lowered independently of the work surface. This action is essential in both clamping or removing a sheet metal workpiece.

The forming bar is designed with a beveled or sloped face so that it will allow sharp bend angles as great as 125 to 135 degrees. Remember that this is the maximum angle that the sheet metal piece will rotate through from its flattened condition. Within the housing, which holds this bar, are two screws sometimes called *setback* adjustments. These screws are used to adjust the forming bar edge up to or back from the fixed table edge. This adjustment of setback from the edge is important and is determined by the thickness of the material being formed. A general rule of thumb for setback is "the thickness of the metal." For stronger or tougher material, the setback may be increased slightly. To adjust the setback prior to forming, one may either use a scale or a piece of the material itself. Always be sure that the setback is the same at both ends of the forming bar.

The forming bar may be removed for replacement or regrinding by loosening its mounting hardware located in the top of its housing mounting. Once the hardware is removed, the forming bar may be slid from the front face of the brake unit.

One more adjustment of extreme importance is the clamping-releasing action of the forming bar. This is the action that is required to clamp and hold a workpiece during its forming. The action is initiated by the lever located at the end of the brake. When this lever is pulled down, a small cam action causes the forming bar to move toward the fixed work plate. This action, when correct, will clamp the workpiece firmly. Due, however, to various gauges of material, it is necessary to adjust this action for positive clamping.

Two large hex nuts, located on the top and at either end of the forming bar holder, supply the necessary adjustment. The procedure for clamping adjustment is a simple operation and follows the preceding steps. First, pull the clamping lever down to its clamping position. Using a piece of stock as a gauge, slide it between the forming bar and the work platen. It is best to do this adjustment at each end. Adjust each nut so that slight contact is felt within the material located between the closed jaws of the brake. Give each nut a one-quarter to one-half turn more for positive clamping. Grasp the material and try to move it. Should it move or slip, adjust the two nuts another one-quarter or one-half turn more. After positive clamping, release the pressure by the clamping handle. Using the handle only, reclamp the workpiece and check it for firmness.

The bend edge of the forming bar is most often designed to produce sharp bends. Bars for producing standard $\frac{1}{16}$- and $\frac{1}{8}$-inch radii are produced, and care should be taken to so note the edge before any bend.

Extending forward and at each end of the main casting are two bearing supports whose function is to support the leaf and handle assembly.

The leaf or apron of the hand brake is the flat steel plate supported for rotation by the end bearings in the main housing. In its normal position, the work face of this plate is in line with the fixed work plate of the main housing. Thus, flat material may be easily inserted or withdrawn without interference. Operation of the leaf handle, however, causes the leaf to rotate about the edge of the work platen and in doing so to form or bend material about the toe or point of the forming bar (see Fig. 6-3).

The amount of foldback or angle of bend of the leaf is controlled by the use of a pin and adjustable stop located at either end of the leaf assembly. Each bearing end of the leaf bar has a series of reamed holes spaced conveniently in an angular pattern. These holes are used to contain hardened dowel pins and act as stops of leaf motion. When installed, these pins will, during motion, contact adjustable stop bars located at the ends of the forming bar. The dowel holes are placed so as to produce

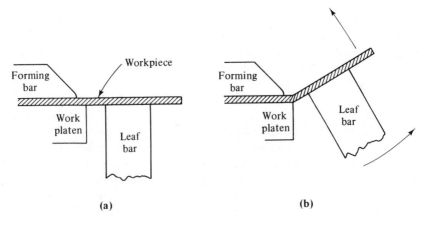

(a)   (b)

Figure 6-3

many of the more required bends, such as 30, 45, 60, and 90 degrees. Metal springback after bending, however, often requires the stops to be adjusted so that a slight overbend initially will produce the required angle. Adjustment of these stops is performed by merely using the screw adjust located at its back end. There are two sets of leaf stops on a brake, but generally only one is used at any one time. Should heavier-gauge material be encountered, both stops should be used.

Bending operations may be performed, after proper setback allowance, by manual alignment and clamping to a layout line or by use of the back gauge adjustable stops.

The use of the gauge stop is preferred when several or many pieces are formed having the same bends and sizes. These gauge stops are made of thin hardened spring steel so that they may operate within the clamping area without interfering with the workpiece clamping. The gauge fingers are attached to a micrometer adjust head at the rear of the brake and thus can be adjusted in increments as small as 0.001 inch.

box fingers and other accessories

In a great many instances, the hand brake is used to close or form the sides of a box from its flat layout. For the performance of this operation, the main forming bar of the brake is removed and replaced with smaller forming bars called *box fingers*. These box fingers are supplied in sets containing various incremental widths that can be built or sized to almost any width. Generally, the size range covers ½ inch to 6 inches, with increments as small as ⅛ inch.

The real purpose of and need for these box fingers can be seen in Fig. 6-4.

Figure 6-4 clearly shows the three stages of producing a closed box: the flat blank, opposite side folds, and, finally, the closing operation.

The reader should see the need for box fingers in the final operation. If one were bending the final two ends of the box, it can be seen that the previously formed sides would interfere with or contact the solid forming bar. This would not allow for a final 90-degree closing. By installing a box finger or a group of fingers so that they lie within the inside size of the box, one can perform a full closing bend.

The fingers are individually secured to the bar holder by using screw hardware. As shown in Fig. 6-4, two gaps are left so that the two previously formed sides will clear and allow a full 90-degree bend to be made.

For forming pieces such as triangular, square, tapered, or rectangular tubes, a special *open-ended* forming bar is available.

In many small box formings, the standard inside corner radius

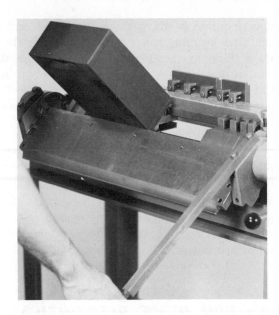

Figure 6-4 — Box fingers in operation. *(Courtesy of DI-ACRO/ Houdaille Industries Inc.)*

most specified is the $\frac{1}{16}$- or $\frac{1}{8}$-inch size. Forming bars with these radii are available from the manufacturer.

To aid in the area of forming sharp angles, seams, and hems an *acute angle bar* is made. This bar will allow a maximum angle of bend to approximately 150 degrees. The acute angle blade is, however, limited to thinner gauge material as compared to the standard sharp bend bar.

The previous discussion of the leaf brake and its accessories is but a theoretical approach. Actual working experience is necessary to solidify these thoughts. When understudying your instructor, be sure to ask questions in those areas of inexperience. Improper use of this or any equipment could cause it to become damaged.

To help ease that first encounter, let us recap some of the basic points. Inspect the forming bar as to whether it is the sharp bend or radius form type. Be sure that the bar is securely fastened. Using either a scale or a piece of the workpiece sheet, adjust the setback of the forming bar edge. With the workpiece or similar ·gauge material, set the clamping pressure as previously discussed.

When forming bends of specific angles, make use of the pin stops located at either end of the leaf bar. To compensate for springback, adjust the stop bars as discussed earlier.

In cases where several pieces of the same shape and bend form are to be made, set the gauge stops to position the sheet. Finally, and most important of all, use scrap test pieces of the form thickness or an extra form to both gauge and check that the final pieces are of the required finished dimensions.

[6-3]
the press brake

When workpiece forms are of such size and shape that they cannot be easily worked on a leaf brake, the press brake is used. This tool is capable of exerting far more forming pressure than the leaf brake. Forming with this type of machine is achieved by the use of preshaped dies, a fixed female or bottom die and a movable male or punch die. Power to move the upper die is supplied by a handle-ratchet setup or in the larger sizes by electrical motors. A typical hand press brake is shown in Fig. 6-5.

The hand press brake is usually designated by three characteristics: its capacity, length of bed, and its forming power. Most of the hand press

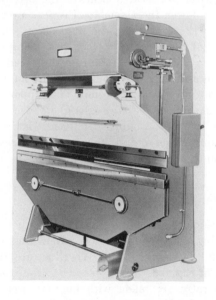

Figure 6-5 — Press brake. *(Courtesy of DI-ACRO/Houdaille Industries Inc.)*

brakes are limited to 16-gauge mild steel sheet. Length of work bed varies as to the size of the brake. Most often the size range begins with a 24-inch and runs to a 48-inch size by 12-inch increments. Forming power, measured in tons, starts in the range of 8 tons for the small press brakes to 35 tons and more on the larger brakes.

The press brake, with its various die forms, will produce simple bends, radius bends, corrugation, flanging, seaming, flattening, and various other bends not formable on the leaf brake.

basics of the press brake

The main housing of the press brake is constructed of either a cast or welded frame. The working end, or front of the machine, contains a bed plate and a movable powered ram. The bed plate is a machined metal bar with a keyway machined across its length. This keyway provides an aligning surface for holding the various die forms used. The bed plate has a series of screws along its face surface, which are used to secure the form die in place.

The bed plate assembly has the ability to be raised or lowered with respect to the main frame. This adjustment is not often used unless a special work form requires this action. Adjustment, if required, is achieved by loosening the main bed plate bolts located along its face. Vertical screw adjustments located beneath the bed plate can then be employed to raise or lower the assembly. Proper lowering or raising is always checked with the top punch die in position. This method eliminates the possibility of the top and bottom dies' being out of alignment. After adjustment, the bed plate screws are retightened.

The upper ram assembly is made so that the hand or powered motion is translated to a up or down motion. This upper ram, like the bed plate, contains a machined keyway along its face. The keyway is machined to accept the top or punch die form. Clamping of the punch is performed by using either individual clamping screws or a clamping bar running the length of the ram face.

press brake dies

Forming dies on press brakes may be of two types: air bending or bottoming dies. Air bending dies are those most often used to produce large-radius bends or full 90-degree bends. To illustrate the theory of air forming, let us look at Fig. 6-6.

The dies generally are made with angular sections less than 90 degrees; as shown in the figure, 85 degrees is the most optimum angular size. In producing large-radius bends, the ram stroke can be set to bring

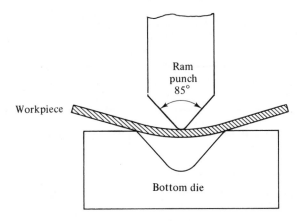

Figure 6-6 — Air forming dies.

pressure along its punch edge and the workpiece so that a bending action is formed with the top edges *A* of the bottom die. This is illustrated in Fig. 6-6(b). Suppose that the need now is to produce a 90-degree bend with these dies. The ram stroke is set to bottom the punch into the bottom die with material allowance considered. In very soft material, it may be necessary to not bottom the punch fully, since one could form an angle of 85 degrees instead of the required 90 degrees. The 85-degree angle of the air dies is designed for those metals that exhibit "springback." Thus, it is necessary to form past the angle and then allow the workpiece to spring back slightly. The final inside radius of a bend using air dies is really determined by the size of the bottom die's major width. The general rule of thumb is to select a bottom die whose opening is eight times the thickness of the metal being formed.

Bottoming dies, unlike air dies, perform their action with tremendous pressure, "coining" or forming the workpiece between the dies. Use of bottoming dies, however, is most often limited to mild steel 12 gauge and under.

Figure 6-7 is included at this time to illustrate some of the more common bottoming dies. The basic forming operation most often associated with any particular die is shown with that die. The hemming die, however, requires two operations. Hemming in sheet metal is essentially the same operation as that performed on cloth.

It is the operation of folding an edge of metal through a 180-degree angle so that it either has a small inner radius or is flattened. Hemming in sheet metal serves two purposes: strengthening an edge and reducing the possibility of edge cuts to future handlers or users of the product.

Dies for the press brake can be obtained in various lengths other

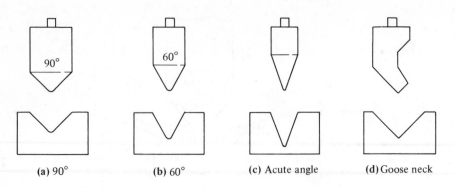

(a) 90°   (b) 60°   (c) Acute angle   (d) Goose neck

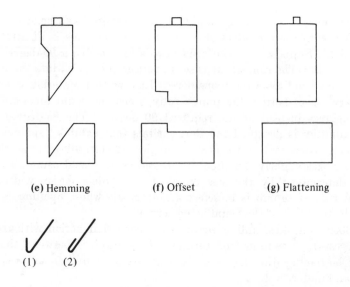

(e) Hemming   (f) Offset   (g) Flattening

(1)   (2)

Figure 6-7 — Dies.

than full-length sections. This is particularly important when punch changes are frequent on small workpieces. Consider the forming of a large box pan with shallow sides. The initial bends can be made with a punch or series of punch forms clamped together on the ram. When closing the box becomes the next operation, the punch sections can be removed so that the remaining section fits inside the nearly completed form and allows the ends to be closed.

rubber dies

Often painted or polished sheet metal sections must be formed without marring or scratching the finish. This operation, when required, can be performed by using a rubber-filled bottom die form and a metal punch of the required shape (Fig. 6-8).

The die block is made of neoprene or urethane rubber contained in a rugged metal holder. Generally, an air gap is located at the bottom of the rubber block and the die holder. This gap is necessary for air to escape during a forming operation, thus preventing excessive wear and tear on the rubber.

Before using a punch on a rubber die, be sure to check the factory specifications concerning maximum gauge and punch penetration limits. This is important, since rubber dies are made to range from very flexible to very hard elasticity. Deep penetration into very hard rubber with sharp punches could damage the rubber pad.

Rubber pads are most often secured to the die holders by use of double-backed adhesive tape and metal end caps. The tape is set in the bottom of the die holder with the rubber pad placed over it. This prevents the strip from popping out during the punch withdrawal. The metal end caps are used to keep the forming pressure of the punch from extruding the rubber at its ends.

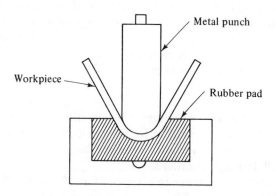

Figure 6-8 — Rubber die forming.

ram—stroke adjustment

After dies are installed on a press brake, one of the first items that must be adjusted is the stroke. In the smaller hand-ratchet types the bottom bed plate can be adjusted and locked to the correct setting, while in others a screw adjust wheel raises or lowers the ram with respect to the bottom die.

In power press brakes, adjustment is much faster and easier than in the hand-powered version. A circular graduated dial is located at the right side of the main press housing. This circular dial has two graduations denoted about its edge. Generally, in the case of a 2-inch stroke, the graduations are indicated from ⅛ inch to 2 inches. The increments past the ¼-inch mark are noted in ¼-inch increments. Two adjustable stops are affixed to this graduated dial. One stop adjusts the down stroke distance, and the second adjusts the upstroke travel. Once set and locked, the stops allow the power press to cycle through selected up and down motions. As the press travels to its "set" down position, that stop trips either an electrical or a hydraulic stop lever to reverse the motion. As the stroke starts up, the second stop comes into action by contacting its own electrical or hydraulic stop lever. This stops the press until the next cycle. On powered press brakes, a foot pedal must be depressed to start the next cycle.

press brake stop gauges

Back stop gauges on press brakes are basically of two forms, both of which are micrometer adjusted. The more basic type is of the form discussed in the section on the hand-operated shear. The larger press brakes, however, have two front adjusting wheels with counters that set stop distances to three decimal places. These gauge stop adjust wheels are located on the front of the bed plate at each end. This dual adjust allows the technician to independently offset each stop to produce or accept tapered or irregular-shaped workpieces.

The press brake is a most useful tool in the metal forming trades. The variety of work produced includes: 90-degree, obtuse, and acute angle bends, large-radius sections, seaming, flanging, reverse bends, corrugation, and flattening operations.

As discussed previously, two types of dies are available, the air die and the bottoming die. The air die is often used in forming large-radius sections or 90-degree bends with minimum pressure. The bottoming dies, used in short- to large-run forming, are made in a wide range of the more common bend forms. Use of bottoming dies requires significantly more forming pressure than the air dies, due to the "coining" action of the punch and die.

When using either die form, remember to set the stroke of the ram to produce the correct bend form. Whenever possible, use either scrap pieces of the material or a test piece to set and prove the stroke and gauge stop sets. Never guess the setup and proceed on the actual workpiece.

In setting the stops on a power press brake, the first operation should be performed on the down ram stroke. This stroke is the motion that performs the required bend. The upstroke can be set to minimize *up* travel, especially important in a large run of work.

[6-4]
slip rollers

Slip rollers are a forming tool whose specific task is to form flat work sheets into cylindrical (circular) sections, large-radius sections, or flat and curved segments. This machine is available in both hand-power or electric motor-driven types.

Grading or size is governed by three parameters: maximum workpiece width, gauge capacity, and diameter of the work rolls. The general size range of these tools is 6-inch–16 gauge–1-inch, 12-inch–16 gauge–2-inch. Figure 6-9 shows a typical hand slip roll machine.

Figure 6-9 — Rubber slip rollers. *(Courtesy of DI-ACRO/Houdaille Industries Inc.)*

basics of the slip roll

The forming operation of the slip roll is produced by three cylindrical and parallel rolls affixed to a housing. The fixed or *power roll* is secured within the end housings of the machine and supplies turning power, either by hand crank or motor power. The *clamping roll,* located above the power roll, is adjustable to accept various gauges of metal. It is the purpose of this clamping roll first to locate a workpiece between itself and the lower power roll and also to provide a limit to the minimum radius bend or cylinder that can be formed. The third roll or *pressure* roll is positioned behind the fixed and clamping roll and is adjustable with respect to the previous working and clamping rolls. It is the purpose of this third roll to apply pressure to the sheet passing through the work rolls so that it curves or forms a radiused bend to the sheet. This three-roll setup is shown in Fig. 6-10.

It can be seen from Fig. 6-10 that, as the pressure roll is adjusted inward to the power and clamping roll, the radius of the sheet will become smaller and smaller. The radius of bend is, however, limited by the diameter of the clamping roll. This is to say that as the pressure roll is adjusted inward, the sheet will be reformed to a smaller and smaller radius until the sheet is formed about the clamping roll diameter.

When a cylindrical section is formed on a slip roll, one's first question is, "How do I remove it from the machine?" The clamping roll is designed with a split bearing at one end that allows the roll to be unclamped and pulled away from the machine. The opposite end of the clamp roll is secured in a bearing that contains the roll end, but pivots about the left side of the main roll housing. This arrangement allows one to slip the formed section from the machine. In many cases, the release

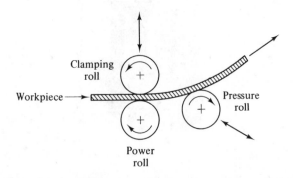

Figure 6-10 — A three-roll setup.

of the clamping roll is performed with either a handle release or a screw nut array.

When sections containing flat and curved segments are to be formed, the cam-actuated pressure or idler roller-equipped machine is used. This arrangement is one in which a cam-adjusted pressure roll is displaced or brought into contact with the workpiece by merely actuating a hand lever. Disengagement allows the work sheet to feed through the work rolls without any forming pressure. When the zone or layout mark of the next required bend radius is encountered, the pressure roll is brought into action by the hand lever, and that radius can then be formed.

basics of slip roll forming

Whether the finished section is to be a cylindrical, a curved, or a conic section, it will in all cases begin with the flat layout pattern of the form. An intermediate step prior to forming may, however, require that the abutting edges be seamed, or have lock joint seams or other such edges. These end bends are best performed prior to the roll forming operation. Either the leaf or press brake is used for straight forming bends.

The prepared sheet may now be placed into the slip roll for the forming operation. Back off both the pressure and forming roll to allow easy entrance of the sheet.

Adjust the clamping roll down to make contact with the sheet; be sure that you do not clamp on an existing seam form.

An operation called "breaking the sheet" is now performed. This merely entails the passing of the sheet through the rolls with little or no pressure from the forming roll. After the sheet has been passed through, it is removed and flipped over so that the opposite side can be "broken." This action of breaking has a tendency to weaken the surface strength of the material and thus to allow it to be flexed or formed into a smooth curved final form.

When sheet products are formed without the breaking operation, the curved surface appears to be formed by a series of bend lines running parallel to the forming rolls.

Cones (truncated) may be formed without too much difficulty by using the slip roll. The smaller opening of the cone, however, must be larger than or equal to the diameter of the pressure roll. Figure 6-11 shows a flat cone layout in the slip rolls.

The theory of forming a cone is that the length A and the length B must pass through the rolls in stepped proportions. This can be shown by the dotted lines of the flat cone in Fig. 6-11. For each incremental length

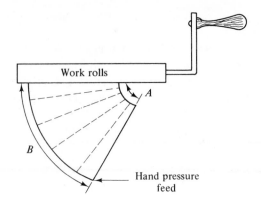

Figure 6-11 — Cone forming on a slip roll (top view).

of *A* that is rolled, a larger proportional length of *B* must be correspondingly formed.

To maintain this proportion, it is necessary to use hand pressure along the larger edge *B* so that the pressure will slide the sheet between the clamping and work rolls. It is important, therefore, to adjust the clamping pressure more at the *A* or small end of the cone with little or no clamping pressure at the *B* or larger end of the cone layout. This form of clamping allows the point *A* to act as a pivot point so that hand control of the *B* edge is easily maintained.

When one is forming, two important points must be remembered. The movement of the forming roll by its screw adjustments should always be done in small parallel increments. This procedure both insures smoothness of curves and also allows accurate sizing of the finished section with respect to radius or diameter. The second point to remember in slip roll forming is never to back a workpiece out while it is in contact with the pressure and forming rolls. Roll mounting looseness, particularly that of the pressure roll, can drastically alter the radius of the workpiece to the point that it can be ruined. If the slip roll is equipped with a cam-operated pressure roll, disengage it from contact with the workpiece during a backout operation.

rod, tube, and bar forming

Circular forms of either rectangular, square or round bar sections may be formed by using the slip roll. The main limitation in forming these sections is the gauge or thickness of the section itself.

Often, grooved work rolls are available to accept the more common shapes such as round and square bars (see Fig. 6-12).

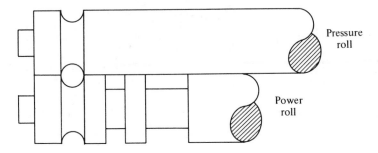

Figure 6-12 — Grooved slip rolls.

For forming round rods or tubing, both the power and pressure roll are grooved. Grooving of both rolls is essential to prevent distorting or flattening of the roundness. In square or rectangular sections, only the power roll is grooved to the actual cross section of the form. The pressure roll is not grooved when square or rectangular sections are formed.

Again, to remove formed round rod or bar sections, the pressure roll is disengaged by means of its release mechanism. This allows the formed section to be removed from the three-roll forming setup.

Several of the more simple bar and rod forms may be formed into circles or large-radius sections by using a slip roll. A bender, however, discussed in the following section, is the more diverse tool used for radius bends when a wide range of shapes and forms is required.

[6-5]
the bender

A basic tool used in the sheet metal trades is the hand or powered bender. This tool is capable of forming a variety of long thin metal products by either "crush" forming or "wiper" forming. Crush forming is merely forming a metal section in which finish and final cross-sectional size is not too important. Bending a metal bar or rod in one's hands can be called crush forming. In bending thin-wall sections, such as tubing, pipe, channels, or other such forms, "wiper" forming dies are used. These dies maintain both the size and form of the workpiece after bending. This is important particularly in tubing, where the flow of a liquid would be restricted if the bend closed the tube. Figure 6-13 is given to illustrate some of the basic forming applications of the bender.

Benders are sized by the maximum radius that can be formed. This range generally falls into four groups: 2-inch, 6-inch, 9-inch, and 12-inch

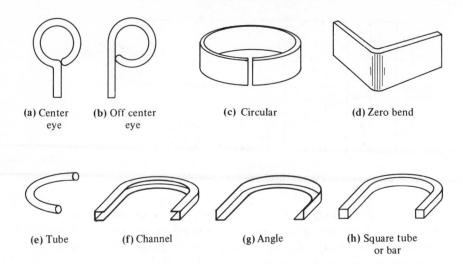

(a) Center   **(b)** Off center   **(c)** Circular   **(d)** Zero bend
eye   eye

(e) Tube   **(f)** Channel   **(g)** Angle   **(h)** Square tube
or bar

Figure 6-13 — Bends.

benders. Material capacity is given in round and square bar, tube, pipe, flat bar (flat and edge) angle, and channel. If any doubt exists concerning the capacity for a particular workpiece, consult the manual supplied by the manufacturer.

basics of the bender

The basic theory of forming as performed on a bender is rather simple. A work table is provided such that it may accept both sized pins and forms about which the workpiece is to be formed. Affixed to the work table, and rotatable about it, is the *nose holder arm*. This arm supplies the forming power to shape the workpiece about the fixed form or radius pin located on the work table. The hand bender is shown in Fig. 6-14.

The work table contains a center pin hole with a spiral pattern of holes located about it. The center hole, which is most important, is used to hold radius pins of various diameters or forming dies such as those that would be used in tube or special-shape forming. The spiral pattern is such that stop or bend point pins can be located. These holes are most often used to form eyes or zero bend pieces, as shown in Fig. 6-13, or merely to locate and lock the end of the workpiece during bending.

The nose holder arm, as previously stated, is designed to deliver power to a nose forming block located at its end. Three basic forms of nose blocks are available and are easily installed in the arm. They are the standard forming nose, the roller nose, and the grooved or specially formed roller nose. The nose former shown in Fig. 6-14 is the standard forming nose.

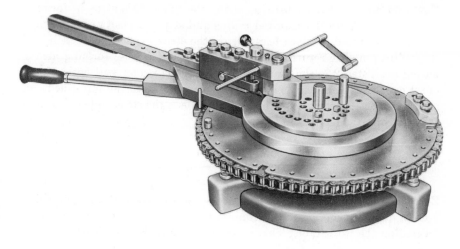

Figure 6-14 — Hand bender. *(Courtesy of DI-ACRO/Houdaille Industries Inc.)*

The forming nose is secured to the main holder arm by an adjustable block. This arrangement allows the nose former to be adjusted to the specific radius pin or form being used on the work table.

A *stock stop gauge* is provided in the nose block assembly to set the proper length of those pieces that must be formed in large numbers. Usually, after several trial and error settings, the stop is located and secured with its locking screw.

Two additional gauges are provided on the bender for repetitive work runs; these are the *return stop* and the *angle gauge stop*. The return stop, located on the circular plate below the main arm, is set at the initial work-pin and nose-form position. This stop will allow one to return to the initial point for second or multipiece formings.

The angle gauge stop is a circular section that is secured to the same table as the return stop pin. Two screws located within its circular slot allow it to be adjusted accurately to any required degree of bend. To summarize, the forming travel of the bender is set to operate between the return stop and the angle stop.

operations of the bender

To illustrate the procedures of several common bends, this section will discuss *centered eyes, zero bends, circular forms,* and tube and channel forming. The formation of other special forms and shapes are most often presented in the manual supplied by the manufacturer.

Centered Eye — Figure 6-15(a) shows the three basic steps in forming centered eyes. With the required radius and stop pin positioned, the nose former is adjusted to place pressure on the stock located between it and the radius pin. The return stop can now be set. The nose forming arm is moved until step 2 in the figure is met. This, the reader will notice, is an offset eye. The final operation is the nose contact with the unformed end of the eye stock. Pressure on this portion causes the stock to bend around the stop pin, thus offsetting it to form the centered eye. The angle stop should be set when the proper offset is defined. With the stock length gauge in the nose arm set, and the return and angle stop set, repeated centered eyes may be produced.

Zero Radius Bending — This operation, most often performed on small rectangular brackets or rods, requires that a preformed angle block be located on the work table. This setup is shown in Fig. 6-15(b). The im-

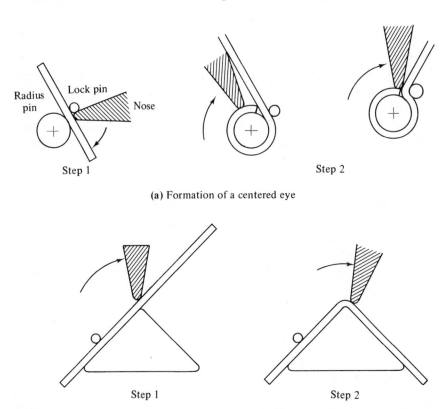

(a) Formation of a centered eye

(b) Zero radius forming

Figure 6-15

portant step in this operation is to set up the nose former to the apex of the block with the stock thickness located between. It is important to position the block apex at the center of the work table so that the nose former will swing in a radial line path about it. Step 1 in Fig. 6-15(b) shows the stock located between the formed block and locking pin. As the nose arm is rotated, it will sweep the stock about and over the apex of the former block. Again, as before, the return and angle stop should be set for repetitive bends.

Circular Forms — Circular forms of either flat, square, or round stock can be produced with ease on the bender. Stock of the required length to form the section is placed between the formed radius block and a stop pin so that about half of the length is on either side of the stop pin. The former arm and nose are used to complete one side of the circular form. The partial form should be removed and placed in the radius block and lock pin so that the remaining straight section can be formed.

Tubing Forming — This operation requires that a preformed and sized block be located on the work table center. A grooved nose roller having the same radius as the workpiece is installed in the former arm. In some instances, a wiper block having the radius can be used and the standard nose roller merely backs it up. The above-mentioned forms are shown in Fig. 6-16.

The forming blocks are designed to produce 180 bends with some allowance for springback. Bends less than 180 degrees are easily performed and reproduced when the return and angle stops are set.

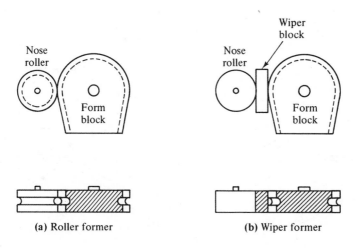

(a) Roller former   (b) Wiper former

Figure 6-16 — Forms.

Not shown but important is a tube end clamp. This mechanism is used to position and clamp the straight tube to the forming block prior to forming.

Channel, Angle, and Square Forming — When forms such as channel, angle, or square forms are bent, the basic design of the forming block is one having a square groove. This square groove maintains the cross-sectional shape of the piece during forming. When channel is formed, the use of a flat backup wiper placed between the nose roller and channel is recommended. In the case of "flanging," the wiper block should bear on the outer leg during forming. This form of bend is shown in Fig. 6-17. In forming angle with the *flange out*, the wiper should bear on the bottom leg of the angle for support. For both channel and flange "in" situations, the forming collar should be machined or formed to accept the inward extensions of the shape. Often forming blocks are available such that they can be assembled to produce the required cross section of "in" formed flanges and shapes.

In summary, the most important points to remember are that the stops, be they stock length, degree, or return, are set on a trial and error basis, because any metal product that is bent or formed has a tendency to spring back after forming. To produce accurately required shapes, this

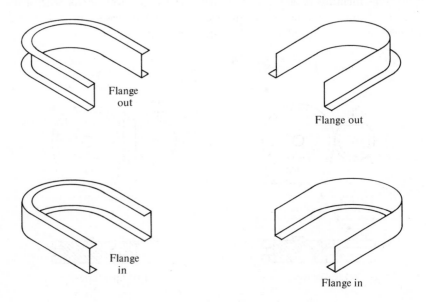

Figure 6-17

springback is first defined by several test pieces. It is only after the test setup that the actual workpieces should be formed by using the preset stops.

review questions

6-1 / Forming sheet metal into various shapes is most often performed on four types of tools. List them and their specific operations (straight bends or curved bends).

6-2 / In what general width range are leaf brakes produced?

6-3 / Leaf brakes most often are used to form 90° bends. They are, however, capable of bends greater or less than 90°. What angles are called *obtuse* and what angles are called *oblique?*

6-4 / Describe a reverse bend. What is a hem?

6-5 / What functions does the forming bar perform in bending operations

6-6 / Define the term *setback* in metal forming. Why is it important?

6-7 / Describe the procedure in setting the clamping–release pressure of the forming bar.

6-8 / The nose of the forming bar can be generally found in either of what two radii?

6-9 / What is the function of the leaf or apron of the brake?

6-10 / The amount of fold back is controlled accurately by two devices. What are they and how are they adjusted?

6-11 / What is *springback?*

6-12 / Box fingers are used in what specific areas of folding?

6-13 / How are the box fingers selected and held in the brake housing?

6-14 / Two special forming bars are made for the brake—the open ended and the acute angle bar. Describe their purposes.

6-15 / Press brakes most often use two types of forming dies. What are these types?

6-16 / How are the forming dies secured to the press brake?

6-17 / What is the most important operation to perform after the installation of the forming dies?

6-18 / How is the ram adjustment set on power presses to controlled up–down operations?

6-19 / What forms of gauge stops are found in press brakes?

6-20 / What is *corrugation* as defined in sheet metal practices?

6-21 / Slip rolls perform operations on several forms. What is the operation and list several forms.

6-22 / What determines the minimum diameter that can be formed on a slip roll?

6-23 / Define *breaking* of a sheet on the slip roll.

6-24 / How is a formed section removed from the roll assembly?

6-25 / A bender uses two methods of forming; name and describe them.

6-26 / What function does the nose block perform on the bender?

6-27 / List the three main stops on the hand bender. What is the purpose of each?

6-28 / Explain *zero* bending. When is it used?

6-29 / What changes must be made on the bender prior to a tube bending operation?

7

sheet metal seams, joints, and fasteners

[7-1]
introduction

In practically all sheet metal fabrications, the securing of ends, edges, or additional sections is most often accomplished by using seam joints or fasteners.

In this chapter we list and describe the more common types of seams and finally list the various types of fasteners used. These fasteners are sheet metal screws, self-tapping screws, standard rivets, expanding rivets, and insert hardware.

[7-2]
seam joints

Seam joints are designed to be employed in thin- to medium-gauge sheet metal assemblies. The use of these joints can be seen in cylindrical sections and a host of other assemblies. The more common seam joints, shown in Fig. 7-1, are secured by three basic operations at their assembly point. They may be hammer peened or flattened; they may be fastened with hardware; in cases where leaktight joints are required, they may be soldered.

The *peened lock* joint, shown in Fig. 7-1(a), is possibly the simplest

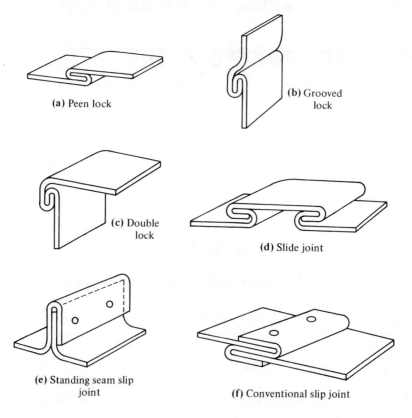

(a) Peen lock

(b) Grooved lock

(c) Double lock

(d) Slide joint

(e) Standing seam slip joint

(f) Conventional slip joint

Figure 7-1 — Seam joints.

joint made in the trades. It can be used effectively in both circular sections or in joining one flat section to another, as in forming a square or rectangular section. Peen lock joints are formed quite easily by using a leaf or press brake. For accurate stock allowance to produce this joint, consult the bend allowance formulas previously given. The inner radius of the joint may or may not be specified on the drawing; however, a good point to remember is that the minimum radius of bend must be equal to or greater than one-half of the material thickness that engages this joint. This rule of thumb is true only when this joint is formed of similar gauge metal.

Final closure of the peened joint is performed with a hammer made of hard rubber or rawhide. The underside of the joint must be backed up with either a flat metal surface or a round metal rod in the case of a cylinder. With the joints engaged, pressure from clamps or a hand should be applied to keep the joints engaged. With a hammer, sufficient force is struck to cause the joints to flatten and lock. This flattening is performed along the entire joint. To further secure the flattened joint from opening, center punch marks are produced at intervals along the joint. This has the effect of producing conical interlocking marks on the underlying sections of the joint. Sheet metal screws or solder may also be used to secure the joint.

The *grooved lock joint* shown in Fig. 7-1(b) is a variation of the simple interlocked peened joint. This joint has a decidedly stronger design and better appearance than the simple peen joint. This joint is used to join sections where it is important that both sections lie in the same plane or line. This is achieved by offsetting the one side of the joint so that the return bend is offset one thickness of its matching gauge joint.

Again, like the simple peen joint, the groove lock is used in joining cylindrical or straight sections where appearance and strength are required. The material allowance necessary to produce the joint should be calculated, the dimensions and given formulas being used. Both the leaf and press brake are used to produce this joint.

The simple peened joint can be turned into a grooved lock joint with the use of a grooving tool. This forming tool has a flat face with a rectangular groove machined across its face. When placed over a peened joint and struck sharply with a hammer, it forms a grooved lock joint.

The *double lock joint* is a seam joint used exclusively on the edge or corner of flat sheet assemblies. Its final shape is shown in Fig. 7-1(b). The design is such that it both strengthens and locks the seam while it excludes any edge roughness or burrs. This joint is used extensively in metal furniture and chassis constructions.

Return briefly to the grooved lock joint, Fig. 7-1(b), and it can be seen that it is the basic joint of the double lock. The only difference is that the one sheet section is formed or peened until it is at an angle of 90 degrees to its original position.

The *slide joint* is a very special form of joint used extensively in duct work and chassis assemblies. It is designed so that two sections with 180-degree folded ends can be secured by sliding a folded and radiused locking strip joining the two sections.

On chassis, this slide joint array can be incorporated in producing covers that are slid in or out of the main frame. This is important where easy access is required to service equipment mounted within the box.

The slide joint can be formed by use of either the leaf or press brake. For accurate fitting, it is required that the stretchout be calculated, the bend radius formulas being used.

The *standing seam slip joint* is another joint used quite often in heating, ventilation, and air conditioning (HVAC) ducts. Its form is simple, and the raised seam offers some rigidity to large unsupported sections.

The joint design is of further importance where noise or sealing gaskets of cloth, rubber, or cork are required. The gasket, when used with this type of joint, is folded over the single standing edge of the one section. The folded edge is then pressed over or slipped to capture the insulating material. Final locking of this joint is, however, achieved by using fasteners of the screw or rivet type.

When forming this simple joint on the leaf or press brake, be sure to allow clearance for the use of insulating material when it is specified. The throat opening of the folded edge should be two times the thickness of the insulator plus the thickness of the engaging single-fold insert. Use of the bend allowance formulas is recommended for calculating the stretchout.

The *conventional slip joint* is a very useful joint in both thin or heavy gauge material [Fig. 7-1(f)]. Its design as illustrated produces a lap-type joint with the flattened ''S'' locking plate. The locking plate serves two purposes: It holds the mating workpiece ends in defined slots and also defines the amount of overlap. This form of joint is designed for heavy pushing or pulling forces exerted on the joint. Again, as with the standing seam slip joint, fastening hardware must be used to secure the final joint. Insulating or sealing gaskets can be used most effectively with this joint form.

The simple attractiveness of this form of joint is in the fact that the workpieces themselves are not formed. This is particularly important where the size or gauge of the metal would make some other configuration of joint difficult to form. The locking plate design can thus be made in long lengths on either the leaf or press brake and can be saw cut to required lengths in the field. In some instances, locking plates are pre-drilled or punched in the stretchout, for ease of field installation. Consult the bend allowance formulas to produce accurately located holes in the stretchout.

[7-3]
fasteners
(types of joints)

Fastening sheet metal with various forms of hardware is performed for several reasons: because the material is sufficiently heavy that bending is impossible, or because the design of the work section must be such that removal of certain sections is important in the final product.

Two forms of hardware most used in fabrication are rivet types and screw types. Figure 7-2 is offered to illustrate some of the more common types of fastened sections found in the sheet metal trades.

[7-4]
rivets (standard)

For years, rivets have been used to produce permanent and often water-tight seals between two metal sections. These sections can be of either thin gauge, such as that used in the aircraft industry, or heavy plate used in the construction of bridges, buildings, or ships.

Rivets are very much like "unthreaded" screws in that they have a head design, a body diameter, and length. In the larger type of rivet, six head styles are produced: *button head, high button head, cone head, pan head, flat top countersunk head,* and *round top countersunk head.* Body sizes of these larger rivets generally range from ½ to 1¾ inches in diameter.

The smaller rivets, which we shall be most interested in, are sized from $\frac{1}{16}$- to $\frac{7}{16}$-inch body diameters. This smaller group of rivets has four basic head designs: *flat head* (tinner's rivets), *countersunk head, button head,* and *pan head* (Fig. 7-3).

Rivets are made of a range of malleable materials such as Monel, copper, aluminum, and steel. These materials allow the rivet to be cold formed by peening using hammer blows.

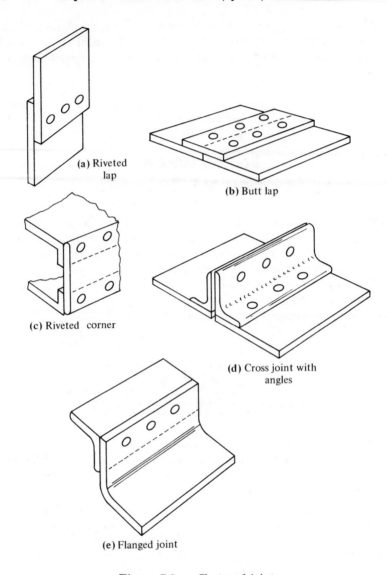

(a) Riveted lap

(b) Butt lap

(c) Riveted corner

(d) Cross joint with angles

(e) Flanged joint

Figure 7-2 — Fastened joints.

Within the small-rivet family, there exists a group whose body diameters range from 0.081 to 0.347 inch. These are graded not by their body diameter, but rather by a number that indicates the average weight of 1000 of those particular rivets.

The procedure of riveting (hand) is basically as follows. A selected rivet is inserted into a common hole existing in two or more pieces. The

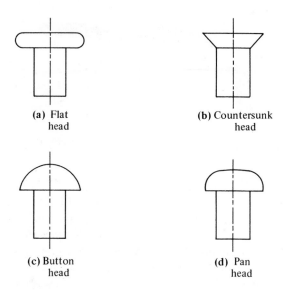

(a) Flat
head

(b) Countersunk
head

(c) Button
head

(d) Pan
head

Figure 7-3 — Basic head designs of small rivets.

rivet length extending from the workpiece should be approximately $1\frac{1}{2}$
to 2 body diameters in length. This length will, of course, depend on the
type of head formed.

With the head backed up firmly with a steel bar or hammer, the
opposite end is peened or formed into a "second" head. Proper formation
is when the material located between the rivet ends is firmly clamped.
To form the second head to a desired shape, a formed tool called a *rivet set*
is used. The preformed cavity in its end will form the rivet end into a
uniformly shaped head.

[7-5]
expanding rivets

Demands within the aircraft and other technical fields making use of the
rivet brought about a design called the expanding rivet. This rivet is used
extensively in areas where access to the back side for forming is impossible. Riveting under such conditions of inaccessibility is called *blind
riveting.*

The makeup of the expanding rivet is essentially two parts, a hollow
rivet with a steel pin or mandrel located within it. Installation of this
type of rivet requires a special hand tool, which is shown in Fig. 7-4.

Figure 7-4 — Hand riveter for expanding types. *(Courtesy of USM Corp., "Pop" Rivet Division)*

The mandrel of the rivet is inserted into the gripper jaws of the tool, where it is held securely. The rivet body is then inserted into the hole located through the workpieces. With hand pressure force holding the rivet head down on the metal, the handles are squeezed until the mandrel breaks from the rivet. Several squeezes may be necessary to achieve mandrel breakaway.

Expanding rivets are available in several head forms, including the 100-degree countersunk head for flush fastening. The diameters available generally include $\frac{3}{32}$, $\frac{1}{8}$, $\frac{5}{32}$, $\frac{3}{16}$, $\frac{7}{32}$, and $\frac{1}{4}$ inch. Rivet material is more commonly produced in Monel, copper, aluminum, steel, and stainless steel. Special types are produced to form water- and pressuretight assemblies.

[7-6]
sheet metal and
self-tapping screws

Sheet metal and self-tapping screws were developed to meet three specific needs in the sheet metal trade : securing thin sheet metal sections together by deforming material at the screw threads, securing a thin-to-thicker section by a self-thread cutting action, and, finally, providing a fast and economical method of fabricating mass-produced consumer items.

Successful use of these types of fasteners is very dependent on a hole of the proper size being provided. Applications of these various screw forms will be listed shortly.

Sheet metal and self-tapping screws have thread forms in two basic styles, screws with coarse high twist threads for thin gauge applications and screws whose size and thread are noted by standard machine screw sizes. Table 7-1 is presented to illustrate the various types of ASA sheet metal/self-tapping screws in general use.

Table 7-1
SHEET METAL/SELF-TAPPING SCREWS

Type	ASA	Manuf.
	AB	AB
	A	A
	B	B
	BP	BP
	C	C
	D	1
	F	F
	G	G
	T	23
	BF	BF
	BT	25
	U	U

For a quick rundown of the forms shown in Table 7-1: Types A, B, BP, and C form threads in the sheet metal by a displacing action. These types are used often in thin gauge metal fastening. Types D, F, G, T, BF, and BT are self-thread cutters. When turned in a proper-sized hole, the end of the fastener will cut its own thread. Type U is a special form used to secure sections permanently and make them tamperproof. These forms are pressed in and can be used in both metal or plastic.

A wide range of head styles is available: pan head, binding head, round head, countersunk head, fillister head, and truss head. Standard screwdriver slots or Phillips styles are also available. When extra turning power is required for assembly, the hex head or hex-head washer type is recommended.

Tables 7-2 through 7-8 are offered to help you select the appropriate fastener for a specific job and then identify the proper hole size required for the specific fastener forms.

Table 7-2
FASTENER SELECTION AND APPLICATION

Type A—used on thin gauge metal, plywood, and asbestos composition materials.

Type B—used on thin to heavy sheet metal, plastics, plywood asbestos composition, and nonferrous metals.

Type BP—same application as type B, but because of cone point, it is used in misaligned hole situations.

Type C—this screw is basically the same diameter and thread series as the machine screw. Used in heavy metal sections, this type is a self-tapping screw.

Types F, G, D, and *T*—thread-cutting types also. These types can be used in aluminum, brass, cast iron, plastics, die castings, and steel.

Types BF and *BT*—thread-cutting types for use in plastics, die castings, resin-type plywoods, and asbestos.

Type U—this type of fastener with its high helix design is pressed into place in both metals and plastics.

Table 7-3
APPROXIMATE HOLE SIZES FOR TYPE A STEEL SELF-TAPPING SCREWS

In steel, stainless steel, monel metal, brass, and aluminum sheet metal

Screw size	Metal thickness	Hole required Drilled or clean punched	Drill size	Screw size	Metal thickness	Hole required Drilled or clean punched	Drill size
4	0.015	0.086	44		0.024	0.113	33
	0.018	0.086	44	8	0.030	0.116	32
	0.024	0.093	42		0.036	0.120	31
	0.030	0.093	42		0.048	0.128	30
	0.036	0.098	40		0.018	0.128	30
6	0.015	0.099	39		0.024	0.128	30
	0.018	0.099	39	10	0.030	0.128	30
	0.024	0.099	39		0.036	0.136	29
	0.030	0.101	38		0.048	0.149	25
	0.036	0.106	36		0.024	0.147	26
7	0.015	0.104	37	12	0.030	0.149	25
	0.018	0.104	37		0.036	0.052	24
	0.024	0.110	35		0.048	0.157	22
	0.030	0.113	33		0.024	0.180	15
	0.036	0.116	32	14	0.030	0.189	12
	0.048	0.120	31		0.036	0.191	11
8	0.018	0.113	33		0.048	0.196	9

Table 7-4
APPROXIMATE HOLE SIZES FOR
TYPE B SELF-TAPPING SCREWS

In steel, stainless steel, monel metal, and brass sheet metal

Screw size	Metal thickness	Hole required	Drill size	Screw size	Metal thickness	Hole required	Drill size
	0.015	0.063	52	8	0.060	0.136	29
	0.018	0.063	52		0.075	0.140	28
	0.024	0.067	51		0.105	0.149	25
2	0.030	0.070	50		0.125	0.149	25
	0.036	0.073	49		0.135	0.152	24
	0.048	0.073	49		0.024	0.144	27
	0.060	0.076	48		0.030	0.144	27
	0.015	0.086	44		0.036	0.147	26
	0.018	0.086	44	10	0.048	0.152	24
	0.024	0.089	43		0.060	0.152	24
4	0.030	0.093	42		0.075	0.157	22
	0.036	0.093	42		0.105	0.161	20
	0.048	0.096	41		0.125	0.169	18
	0.060	0.099	39		0.135	0.169	18
	0.075	0.101	38		0.164	0.173	17
	0.015	0.104	37		0.024	0.166	19
	0.018	0.104	37		0.030	0.166	19
	0.024	0.106	36		0.036	0.166	19
	0.030	0.106	36		0.048	0.169	18
6	0.036	0.110	35	12	0.060	0.177	16
	0.048	0.111	34		0.075	0.182	14
	0.060	0.116	32		0.105	0.185	13
	0.075	0.120	31		0.125	0.196	9
	0.105	0.128	30		0.135	0.196	9
					0.164	0.201	7
	0.018	0.113	33		0.030	0.185	13
	0.024	0.113	33		0.036	0.185	13
	0.030	0.116	32		0.048	0.191	11
7	0.036	0.116	32		0.060	0.199	8
	0.048	0.120	31		0.075	0.204	6
	0.060	0.128	30	$\frac{1}{4}$	0.105	0.209	4
	0.075	0.136	29		0.125	0.228	1
	0.105	0.140	28		0.135	0.228	1
	0.024	0.116	32		0.164	0.234	$\frac{15}{64}$
8	0.030	0.120	31		0.187	0.234	$\frac{15}{64}$
	0.036	0.120	31		0.194	0.234	$\frac{15}{64}$
	0.048	0.128	30				

Table 7-5
APPROXIMATE HOLE SIZES FOR TYPE C STEEL SELF-TAPPING SCREWS

In sheet steel

Screw size	Metal thickness	Hole required	Drill size	Screw size	Metal thickness	Hole required	Drill size
4–40	0.037	0.093	42	10–32	0.075	0.173	17
	0.048	0.093	42		0.105	0.177	16
	0.062	0.096	41		0.134	0.177	16
	0.075	0.0995	39	12–24	0.037	0.189	12
	0.105	0.101	38		0.048	0.1935	10
	0.134	0.101	38		0.062	0.1935	10
6–32	0.037	0.113	33		0.075	0.199	8
	0.048	0.116	32		0.105	0.199	8
	0.062	0.116	32		0.134	0.199	8
	0.075	0.122	3.1mm	$\frac{1}{4}$–20	0.037	0.221	2
	0.105	0.125	1/8		0.048	0.221	2
	0.134	0.125	1/8		0.062	0.228	1
8–32	0.037	0.136	29		0.075	0.234	A
	0.048	0.144	27		0.105	0.234	A
	0.062	0.144	27		0.134	0.236	6mm
	0.075	0.147	26	$\frac{1}{4}$–28	0.037	0.224	5.7mm
	0.105	0.1495	25		0.048	0.228	1
	0.134	0.1495	25		0.062	0.232	5.9mm
10–24	0.037	0.154	23		0.075	0.234	A
	0.048	0.161	20		0.105	0.238	B
	0.062	0.166	19		0.134	0.238	B
	0.075	0.1695	18	$\frac{5}{16}$–18	0.037	0.290	L
	0.105	0.173	17		0.048	0.290	L
	0.134	0.177	16		0.062	0.290	L
10–32	0.037	0.1695	18		0.075	0.295	M
	0.048	0.1695	18		0.105	0.295	M
	0.062	0.1695	18		0.134	0.295	M

Table 7-6
APPROXIMATE HOLE SIZES FOR TYPES D, F, G, AND T STEEL SELF-TAPPING SCREWS

Screw size	Stock thickness										
	0.050	0.060	0.083	0.109	0.125	0.140	3/16	1/4	5/16	3/8	1/2
	Hole sizes in steel										
2–56	0.0730	0.0730	0.0730	0.0730	0.0760	0.0760					
3–48	0.0810	0.0810	0.0820	0.0860	0.0860	0.0860	0.0890				
4–40	0.0890	0.0890	0.0935	0.0960	0.0980	0.0980	0.1015				
5–40	0.1060	0.1060	0.1060	0.1065	0.1094	0.1100	0.1160	0.1160			
6–32	0.1100	0.1130	0.1160	0.1160	0.1160	0.1200	0.1250	0.1250			
8–32	0.1360	0.1405	0.1405	0.1440	0.1440	0.1470	0.1495	0.1495	0.1495		
10–24	0.1520	0.1540	0.1610	0.1610	0.1660	0.1695	0.1730	0.1730	0.1730	0.1730	
10–32	0.1590	0.1660	0.1660	0.1695	0.1695	0.1695	0.1770	0.1770	0.1770	0.1770	
12–24		0.1800	0.1820	0.1875	0.1910	0.1910	0.1990	0.1990	0.1990	0.1990	0.1990
1/4–20			0.2130	0.2188	0.2210	0.2210	0.2280	0.2280	0.2280	0.2280	0.2280
1/4–28			0.2210	0.2280	0.2280	0.2340	0.2344	0.2344	0.2344	0.2344	0.2344
5/16–18				0.2770	0.2770	0.2813	0.2900	0.2900	0.2900	0.2900	0.2900
5/16–24				0.2900	0.2900	0.2900	0.2950	0.2950	0.2950	0.2950	0.2950
3/8–16					0.3390	0.3390	0.3480	0.3580	0.3580	0.3580	0.3580
3/8–24					0.3480	0.3480	0.3580	0.3580	0.3580	0.3580	0.3580

Table 7-7
APPROXIMATE HOLE SIZES FOR TYPES BF, BG, AND BT STEEL SELF-TAPPING SCREWS

Stock thickness	Screw size										
	2–32	3–28	4–24	5–20	6–20	8–18	10–16	12–14	$\frac{1}{4}$–14	$\frac{5}{16}$–12	$\frac{3}{8}$–12
	Hole sizes in zinc and aluminum die castings										
0.060	0.0730	0.0860									
0.083	0.0730	0.0860									
0.109	0.0760	0.0860	0.0980								
0.125	0.0760	0.0860	0.0995	0.1110	0.1200	0.1490	0.1660	0.1910	0.2210	0.2810	0.3438
0.140	0.0760	0.0890	0.0995	0.1130	0.1200	0.1490	0.1660	0.1910	0.2210	0.2810	0.3438
3/16		0.0890	0.0995	0.1130	0.1200	0.1490	0.1660	0.1910	0.2210	0.2810	0.3438
1/4			0.1015	0.1160	0.1250	0.1520	0.1695	0.1960	0.2280	0.2810	0.3438
5/16					0.1250	0.1520	0.1719	0.1960	0.2280	0.2900	0.3438
3/8							0.1719	0.1960	0.2280	0.2900	0.3438

Table 7-8
APPROXIMATE HOLE SIZES FOR TYPE U HARDENED STEEL METALLIC DRIVE SCREWS

In ferrous and non-ferrous castings, sheet metals, plastics, plywood (resin-impregnated) and fiber

Screw size	Hole size	Drill size	Screw size	Hole size	Drill size
00	0.052	55	8	0.144	27
0	0.067	51	10	0.161	20
2	0.086	44	12	0.191	11
4	0.104	37	14	0.221	2
6	0.120	31	5/16	0.295	M
7	0.136	29	3/8	0.358	T

[7-7]
inserted fasteners

Other than the wide range of *add-on* commercial hardware, such as hinges, handles, door knobs, one-quarter turn panel locks, and others, there is a special item very often required in chassis work. This item is a standard machine screw nut used to attach panels, covers, or other items with standard machine screws. This nut, used on thin gauge sections with flanges, is secured to the section in one of several methods. The nut may be held in place via a spring clamp, or it may be pressed or riveted to the metal section. The more commonly used types are illustrated in Fig. 7-5.

The *spring clip nut* is used where alignment of mating parts is somewhat ill-defined. The spring clip itself is composed of a top clearance hole with small projections that engage and locate loosely within the sheet metal flange hole. The lower section of the spring clip contains a standard machine screw nut. Installation is a relatively quick operation, once the proper hole in the sheet metal section is drilled. The diameter of the hole is specified by the manufacturer and varies from size to size. If this information is not available on the blueprint or drawing, the manufacturer's catalog should be used. To install the spring clip nut, merely spring the jaws apart slightly and allow the sheet section to enter. Push the clip slowly to the hole until the locking tabs snap into the hole.

Riveted nuts are installed with minimum time and special tooling. Use of this kind of fastener, however, requires some degree of part align-

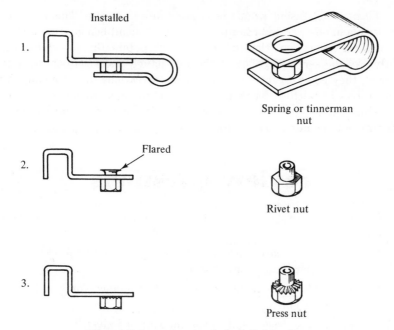

Figure 7-5 — Commonly installed hardware.

ment since they will not move side to side after installation as the spring nut will.

Two factors are considered in selecting these fasteners: thread size and material thickness. Thread size is merely the nut thread size, such as 4-40, or ¼-20. The material thickness is important, since the rivet cuff length of this fastener is specified as to the material thickness on which it is used.

Installation requires that a sized hole be produced. The size for a particular nut will be given on the blueprint or drawing, or determined from the manufacturer's catalog. On the sheet metal face opposite the nut, a small 100-degree countersink can be formed.

Insert the nut cuff from the far side of the countersink. Using either a factory tool punch or the ball end of a peen hammer, strike the extended cuff until it flares and secures the nut from rotation. Excess cuff may be dressed with a file to produce a flush mounting surface. *Press nuts* are distinguished from rivet nuts by the shorter cuff length, which is grooved or splined. In some types, a tooth ring running about the back face of the nut body is employed. Again, as with riveted nuts, thread size and material thickness must be known. The size of the hole required is either specified on the blueprint or drawing, or obtained from the manufacturer's catalog.

This type of fastener must be pressed into the metal. This is usually done with a hand-operated plier press or with a small bench press. During the pressing operation, the cuff of the nut enters the predrilled hole tightly. As the serrated edges of the nut flange make contact with the material, they begin to form corresponding serrations in the metal. This action forces metal to form in the groove of the cuff, forming a locking ring. Thus, the locking ring holds the nut in the material and the serrations prevent the nut from rotating.

review questions

7-1 / List the six basic seam joints encountered in sheet metal operations.

7-2 / What are the basic means of fastening sheet metal sections together, other than seams or welds?

7-3 / Is it necessary to calculate the bend allowance for simple sheet metal seam joints?

7-4 / What are the basic head forms for tinner's rivets?

7-5 / In general, what amount of rivet body should extend from the workpiece prior to riveting?

7-6 / Define *blind riveting*. What tool is available to perform this operation?

7-7 / Select a sheet metal screw for each of the following situations: (a) securing plastic sections; (b) fastening heavy gauge aluminum; (c) heavy gauge copper sheet assembly.

7-8 / Nuts are secured to sheet metal sections most often by what three methods?

7-9 / When a drawing specifies a certain type of insert nut and does not offer the required hole size to receive it, what should your action be?

7-10 / What is the visual difference between a rivet–nut and a press nut?

8

bonding by welding, soldering, and brazing

[8-1]
introduction

Sheet metal products are often fastened together or finished by welding, soldering, or brazing operations. The choice for one of these above methods may be either for pressure- and liquid-tight seams, for overall strength as compared to screws or rivets, or for pure esthetics. In the finished product, where a joint or seam is filled with weld material and dressed with either a grinder or file, the end result appears as if the section were formed of one piece of metal.

Most modern furniture designers make use of welded and ground tubing sections. A quick glance at several pieces of metal office furniture will bear this common practice out.

This chapter will not attempt to teach the precise details of all these methods of bonding, but rather will give the reader adequate knowledge of the more basic forms.

[8-2]
theory of
metal bonding

The bonding of metals of similar or dissimilar nature by welding, soldering, or brazing demands three basic prerequisites: heat, flux, and a filler metal. When these three are present, the bonding process may begin.

Let us discuss this action and arrive at some understanding. Figure 8-1 shows two plates whose beveled ends form a vee-shaped groove when in mutual contact.

Bonding of plate 1 to plate 2 requires that a metal filler material be placed between the two plates so that it adheres to the plate ends and fills the void to produce a completed joint as strong or almost as strong as a single plate.

Adhesion of the filler material is achieved by two methods, *fusion* and *surface adhesion*. The first method, fusion, requires that sufficient heat be supplied to the work area to bring the metal to a plastic or fluid state. The placement of a filler material into this heated fluid area melts the filler rod and intermixes the metals at the welding area. As soon as the heat is removed, the mixed or fused metal weld joint solidifies and hardens. It can then be dressed smooth with either a grinder or a file.

Fusion welding is a process that generates very high temperatures,

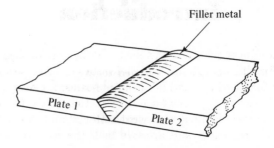

Figure 8-1 — Vee-shaped groove.

which makes it impractical to weld such metals as brass, or plated steel such as tin, galvanized cadmium, etc. Brass and plated steels, when subjected to extremely high temperatures, give off poisonous gases due to the incineration of the plating. In the case of brass, the heat causes migration of alloys within the metals, such as lead.

Surface adhesion bonding, the principle employed in soldering or brazing, is of a low-temperature nature. Bonding is achieved not by fusion, but rather by an adhesion or bonding of the filler metal with the metal surface molecules. It should be obvious that this form of bonding is in many cases not as strong as a fusion-made joint.

Low-temperature bonding is performed on a host of items that have either a low melting point or where fusion welding would prove difficult or impossible.

In practically all metal bonding processes, two factors affect the adhesion or fusion of a filler to the workpiece. These elements are the surrounding air and the cleanliness of the workpiece surface. Air is possibly the worst factor in high-temperature welding, since the combination of heat with air forms a powerful oxidizer. If unprotected, a molten area of weld could burn to a carbonatious or crystalline state with little or no strength.

The second factor that affects bonding, particularly in the lower temperature range, is surface cleanliness. Rust, grease, oils, or other surface contaminants greatly retard the adhesion of the metal filler and the workpiece.

To combat these two elements, the use of a *flux* is often recommended. The fluxing material is used in the immediate area during bonding. It provides protection from air oxidation and, in some cases, cleans the metal surface of contaminants.

The types of filler material have not been discussed at this time, since each bonding process has unique types for a specific process.

[8-3]
TIG (tungsten inert gas) welding

Tungsten Inert Gas (TIG) welding is possibly the most employed type of fusion welding performed on sheet metal products.

The basic source of heat in this process is a controlled electrical arc. A control panel regulates the amount of electrical "heat" or amperes generated at the torch or tip end. This is important, since welding can be performed on a wide range of metal thicknesses without burning the metal.

Let us now discuss the operation of TIG welding. This basic operation is shown in Fig. 8-2.

The hand piece shown in Fig. 8-2 is the heat and flux provider of the process. The electrical power from the control unit is such that a circuit is completed by placing the ground lead to the workpiece, while the hand piece, wired to the controller, forms the other part of the circuit. A tungsten electrode is located at the working end of the hand piece. When the controller is properly set, near contact of the tungsten electrode and the workpiece will cause an arc to form. This arc is the source of heat. As an "air protecting flux," an inert gas such as Argon is passed through the hand piece and exits, forming a protective envelope around the arc.

Filler material in the form of a rod or coil can then be fed through this envelope into the heated arc region. Fusion welding of high quality can now be performed. Selection of the type of filler rod is determined by type of material, thickness, and composition.

Since the "heat" of the arc is controllable, TIG welding lends itself well to welding very thin sheet metal sections. The continuous welding of corner seams or edges of chassis or other such products is often performed with this process.

Use of a filler rod is not essential to every fusion weld operation. In some instances, the two pieces to be jointed are so designed as to allow part of the one piece to melt and fuse with its neighbor. This "no filler" weld operation is illustrated in Fig. 8-3.

Figure 8-3(a) shows a tube section inserted through a plate with a small length of the tube allowed to extend past it. Figure 8-3(b) shows the extension welded (fused) back and into the plate. This welding operation has used the metal tube wall as filler material at the weld joint.

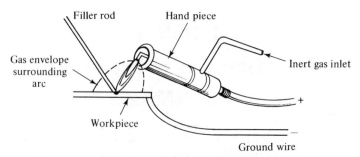

Figure 8-2 — TIG welding process.

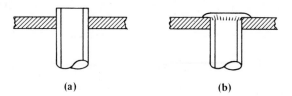

(a)   (b)

Figure 8-3 — "No filler" weld operation.

Before discussing the operation of spot welding, let us look at Fig. 8-4 for some of the more basic types of weld joints encountered in metal fabrication.

[8-4]
the spot welder

The spot welder is a device that may be portable or bench-mounted. Its function is to fuse metal sections together through one or a series of circular weld spots. The actual weld spots are of the fusion type, whereby metal from both sections blends and fuses together.

This form of fastener is used extensively to quickly and effectively bond metal shapes, flats, or other forms together. Most, if not all, of the metal appliances make use of this bonding method. The automobile industry uses the process routinely to assemble, secure, and build the many formed subsections of the vehicle.

The process of spot welding is performed by the action of two factors: clamping or electrode pressure and electrical power pulses. Figure 8-5 shows the typical setup of a spot welder.

Two copper electrodes are electrically tied to an adjustable power supply. The bottom electrode is fixed by screw or clamping pressure to its support arm. The top electrode is movable in an up-and-down stroke with respect to the fixed electrode. Up-and-down motion is achieved through a foot pedal or with hand squeezing pressure. This movable action is important as a means of clamping the workpieces accurately and firmly between the electrodes prior to the spot welding. The pulse of current through the electrodes and workpieces is controlled by an adjustable pressure switch. This pressure switch is set on a trial and error basis until the combination of point pressure and current fuses the metal pieces located between the weld tips. Once a weld pulse is triggered, the tips must be relaxed to perform a second weld pulse.

Weld joint   Symbol

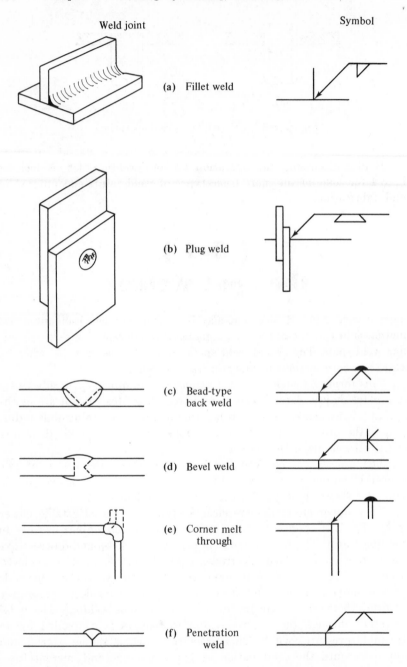

(a) Fillet weld

(b) Plug weld

(c) Bead-type
     back weld

(d) Bevel weld

(e) Corner melt
     through

(f) Penetration
     weld

Figure 8-4 — Basic weld joints and symbols.

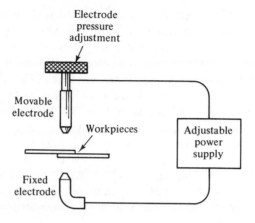

Figure 8-5 — Spot welding arrangement.

The actual process is rather simple. First and foremost, the metal sections must be perfectly clean at the weld points. Flux is never used in this operation, since almost all of the air at the weld point is squeezed out by the electrode clamping pressure. At the instant the electrical pulse is released, the metal immediately under the electrodes is heated to a fusion state. Pressure from the movable tip now forces the semi-molten spot to blend or fuse together, forming a spot weld. This process does leave shallow round depressions in the metal at the point of weld. These depressions, often called "cat heads," are caused by electrode pressure at the instant of welding.

Adjustment of both the watts or watt seconds (power) and the point firing pressure is performed on a trial and error basis. Test pieces should be welded and tested for strength by pulling or twisting them apart. On long-run spot welding, it is good practice to perform this test at regular intervals. This will insure spot welds of uniform strength.

[8-5]
soldering

Soldering is possibly one of the oldest forms of bonding still used. This process is especially well applied to such metals as copper, brass, tinned and galvanized sheet steel, and stainless steels. Soldering of aluminum is possible with the newer forms of aluminum solders. Aluminum-soldered joints, however, are not often encountered in the trades.

The basic solder most used is the tin-lead combination. Variations of this alloy and small amounts of bismuth provide a wide range of melting temperatures to both simplify and ease its application.

Heat to perform this action is mostly supplied from an electrically heated soldering iron or from a propane gas torch. The soldering iron is best used for small areas or workpieces such as wire or thin metal sections. Larger sections, requiring more heat, are best handled by the gas propane torch.

Flux is a must in all soldering operations. It may consist of rosin, muriatic acid, or one of the commercially blended fluxing liquids. Rosin is used exclusively in forming all solder joints in electrical wiring or printed circuit boards. Use of acid-type fluxes is never used in these applications, as residual acid can and does attack delicate wiring and components.

Solder with a rosin core is manufactured. It may be of a single-core or of a multicore type. This arrangement allows the solder with its rosin flux to be used directly on the workpiece. After the joint has been made, the excess rosin is found to form a hard shell on the outer surface of the joint. It can be removed either by scraping or with commercial flux removers.

Liquid fluxes are in most cases brushed onto the pieces prior to heating. It both cleans greases and dirt from the surface and allows for good adhesion of the solder. After any soldering operation with a flux, it is a good idea to clean the excess from the work area.

[8-6]
principles of soldering

Soldering often consists of fillet soldering and lap sweat soldering. Fillet soldering is the process of filling or forming a radius at the corner of two workpieces for both strength and beauty. Lap or sweat soldering is the process of filling the void or space existing between overlapping sheets or tubes. These types are shown in Fig. 8-6.

"Tinning" is the term used to describe the precoating of solder to a workpiece prior to a final assembly. This act insures good adhesion to areas otherwise hidden during assembly and also forms a path into which extra solder may be flowed for a final joint.

Before tinning, the area to be joined should be cleaned with either a wire brush or a piece of steel wool. After cleaning a coating of flux is applied to the area.

In the case of the soldering iron, the tip is fluxed and coated with a

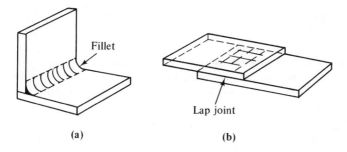

Figure 8-6 — Common solder joints.

layer of solder to insure good heat transfer and also to carry a small amount of solder to the area to be soldered. Hold the iron in one spot until the metal beneath it begins to tin. With a slow back-and-forth motion, begin to travel along the area, feeding new solder to the tip. The idea here is to put down as thin a coat of solder as possible. This is done to both pieces at their joint area. When one is joining larger sections of pipe and tubes, this tinning action is performed best with a gas torch. To move the melted solder over the area, a stainless steel brush is used. Dipping the brush in a flux and then wiping the molten area results in thin, well-made tinned areas.

With pretinning completed, either fillet or sweat joints can be made. Fillet joints are best made by placing the corner down on a work table and flowing solder into the corner. This will result in a radiused fillet, as shown in Fig. 8-6. In sweating a joint, the two pretinned pieces are assembled and heated. As the tinning begins to melt, solder is applied to the corner or edge of the joint. It will be noticed that the new solder is drawn into the heated joint. After the joint area has been loaded, the flame of the torch should be wiped across or around the area to blend and produce a fully sealed joint.

After cooling, clean all the flux from the assembly with either hot soap and water or a flux neutralizer.

[8-7]
brazing

Brazing is the high-temperature process of soldering. The bonding in this process is of the surface adhesion type with no fusion. Two main forms of brazing are most often used: standard brazing (with brass filler rod) and silver brazing.

Standard brazing is an excellent method of joining with good strength such items as plate, angle, bar rod, or other heavy metal sections. Cast iron, which is very nearly impossible to weld or solder, is easily brazed by gas brazing.

Heat for this process is supplied normally from oxygen-acetylene tanks. These gases, when burned at the torch tip, produce the extremely high temperatures required for heating the work and melting the brazing rod.

Flux for brazing consists of a borax combination in a dry form. This flux cleans and protects the heated work area from oxidizing. The flux may be applied independently or may be contained on the filler rod itself.

In general, heating of the workpiece requires that it almost begin to glow to a dull red heat before brazing. At the higher temperature, the white flux powder turns into a clear liquid film under which the melted filler rod will flow and adhere. The spread of the braze over the work area is performed by moving the rod itself in a sweeping back-and-forth motion.

Brazing is often used to build up a worn surface, slot, or hole so that it may be remachined to its original size and shape. After a braze joint has been completed, do not attempt to cool it by use of water. This could cause serious cracks or flaws to develop.

Filler rod compositions are available in a wide range of materials to meet the requirements of strength, corrosion resistance, and temperature. The manufacturer of this product should be consulted for his complete line of filler rods in brazing.

Silver brazing is exactly the same process as standard brazing, but is superior in two areas. Silver-brazed sections are much stronger in the final assembly than those of standard brazing. The nature of the base metal is such that it will, when bonded to the workpiece, follow the hot spot produced on the workpiece by the torch. This then allows the brazing metal to be drawn and spread by the flame tip of the torch. Circular fillet welds or sweat joints can be produced by slowly moving the torch flame along the weld area and feeding filler material just slightly behind it.

Flux for silver brazing is specially designed for this material and is made in either a dry or paste form.

The joint areas must be fluxed prior to brazing. At operating temperature, the flux becomes a clear thick fluid which allows melted silver wire to adhere to the metal surfaces beneath.

Silver braze wire is expensive because of its silver content. It can be obtained in either a silver or brass color. This color range is important if the metal joint is left exposed and must blend in with the surrounding metal finish. Wire diameters can be obtained in $\frac{1}{32}$-inch, $\frac{3}{64}$-inch, $\frac{1}{16}$-inch, and $\frac{3}{32}$-inch sections. It is sold by weight.

To aid in complex assemblies that must be brazed, a wide range of melting temperatures is available. This is very important, so that previous joints will not be melted or weakened by a secondary brazing operation.

Silver brazing can be used successfully in joining common steels, stainless steels, brass, copper, nickel, and tungsten carbide. Tungsten carbide is the material used in masonry drills and cutting tool bits. Silver brazing cannot be used on aluminum or cast iron products.

[8-8]
dip brazing

Dip brazing is a process of creating solid, leaktight joints and seams on very thin to medium gauge aluminum assemblies. Units having many partitions, passages, or other complex forms can be brazed into almost solid formed units by this process.

The part design and its subpieces are fabricated with small tab locks and holes to receive them. The basic assembly of the part is achieved by inserting these tabs into their related holes and twisting them. This action is used to achieve and hold the final shape of the workpiece.

The part is then prepared for dip brazing by cleaning the surfaces of oil, grease, layout fluid, or other foreign material. Small hooks are attached to the part so that it can be held or moved about with some ease.

The aluminum assembly is now immersed into a molten salt bath that contains a flux. The part is allowed sufficient time to bring it to the operating temperature of the bath. Immediately after its removal from the bath, a special aluminum brazing rod is used to "wipe" the seams and joints. The rod, in contact with the flux and heated part, melts and flows along the corners and seams to form a perfect fillet braze.

This process is used only on aluminum assemblies of complex shapes where TIG welding is not practical.

review questions

8-1 / What is the main purpose of brazing, welding, or soldering sections for assembly?

8-2 / In welding, brazing, and soldering, what three things are necessary?

8-3 / What two forms are used for bonding metal to metal products? Explain the differences between the two processes.

8-4 / Why should fusion welding not be used on brass or plated products?

8-5 / What two preparations must be made prior to fusion or adhesion bonding?

8-6 / What is the purpose of a flux?

8-7 / Explain the operation of TIG welding. Does a filler metal have to be used in all cases?

8-8 / The spot welder employs two actions to produce a weld. What are they? What type of bond is produced?

8-9 / Is a flux used in spot welding operations? Explain.

8-10 / A print states that "minimum cat heads" are to be produced at spot welding. Explain.

8-11 / Soldering is most often performed on thin sections of what types of metal?

8-12 / Heat for soldering is supplied by what two basic methods?

8-13 / Is flux necessary in soldering? What type should be used on electronic wiring assemblies?

8-14 / List the two forms of solder joints most often encountered.

8-15 / What is the purpose of *pretinning?*

8-16 / Why is the solder iron tip fluxed and tinned before using?

8-17 / What two general types of brazing are in common use? What heat source is used?

8-18 / What common form of flux is used in brazing operations?

8-19 / Silver braze material can be made to follow curves, lines, edges, etc. How is this achieved?

8-20 / Dip brazing is a process limited to what one metal? Describe the basic operation of dip brazing.

9

sheet metal finishing

[9-1]
introduction

Sheet metal, as supplied by the manufacturer or as fabricated by various shop practices into finished products, is often given a final surface finish. The finish may be decorative or, in special cases, protective in nature.

The purpose of this chapter is to list, define, and acquaint the reader with the more common types and forms of metal finishes. These metal finishes can be said to lie in three groups: bare finishes, painted finishes, and plated or anodized finishes.

[9-2]
bare finishing
of metal

The bare finishing of metal products is, in reality, the reworking of the metal surface itself to produce a wide range of luster or grain. To produce the wide range of bare surface finishes, several techniques are employed.

In general, the range of bare surface finishes includes: *polishing, graining, shot or sand blasting,* and in some special cases *engine lapping.* All of these finishes make use of an abrasive material to produce the desired surface.

polishing

Polishing metals is most often employed for a decorative glossy surface. Most, if not all, metals may be polished by using a fine grinding material called buffing compounds. This material, supplied in block or stick form, is compounded for specific metals that have varying degrees of hardness. This is to say that there are compounds for specifically polishing brass, copper, aluminum, silver, stainless steels, and cold rolled steel.

The process of polishing is performed with two items, a soft cotton disc composed of many circular plys sewn together for thickness, and a polishing compound. The cotton disc, called the *buffing wheel,* is mounted on an arbor of a motor or drill press and is rotated at a speed of from 1750 to 2000 rpm. The polishing compound is then charged or impregnated on the periphery of the rotating buffer. Once the buffer is charged or coated, contact with the metal surface to be polished can be made. The workpiece, held in the hands, is pressed firmly to the rotating buffer with a back-and-forth motion. This motion is necessary to work the surface of the metal to the required luster. Polishing compound charged on the buffer is in some cases rapidly used up, and recharging at regular intervals may be necessary to complete the task. When flat sections are polished, a fixed direction of buffing should be maintained. This is to say that one should not *cross buff* a finished surface, as this will cause a dulling or marring of the finish. When a workpiece is initially buffed to the required luster, the final operation should be the passing of the buffer rapidly along the entire surface in straight overlapping passes. This will polish out or blend short patchy sections from previous buffings and give the surface a uniform polish.

To make buffing both safe and successful, the following suggestions are made. The metal piece should be cleaned of grease, dirt, or rust. Large scratches or burrs should be worked out with emery paper. Remember, polishing will not remove scratches or burrs; it will merely polish them. Select the proper compound for the metal being polished. After buffing, excess compound adhering to the work surface may be removed with kerosene. A soft rubbing action with a dampened cloth is the best approach.

For safety, always wear gloves and a full-face safety shield. Be extremely careful of sharp edges, corners, or other surface features of the workpiece that may catch on the buffing wheel.

graining

Graining is a surface finish most often applied to metal surfaces that will be left as is, coated with a clear lacquer or plastic, or prepared for aluminum anodizing. Anodizing of aluminum will be discussed later in this chapter. Generally, brass, aluminum, stainless steel, or other non-oxidizing metals are grained.

Graining of metal is often specified on a sketch or print with two notations: *grain size* and *direction of lay*. The grain size is a number that corresponds to a grit size of emery. For example, a grain rating of 100 would mean that an emery paper grit of size 100 would be used. The term *lay* merely shows the direction in which the graining or paper must move in order to produce the final grain pattern.

Graining may be performed with either a hand stroking action or a power-driven belt sander. In either case, the lay must be in one direction as specified.

Hand graining of small pieces is most easily performed with a sheet of emery wrapped around a block of wood. Never use a block of material other than wood, as it can rub and scratch the metal being grained.

Hold the block with both hands and stroke in full-length straight strokes. Try to keep the grain pattern as straight and even as possible. Frequent replacement of the emery is helpful in producing an even grain pattern. To inspect the finish it is very important to wash the surface with kerosene or soap and water. Inspect the evenness of the graining, and restroke or blend if necessary.

shot and sand blasting

Shot or sand blasting is a process used extensively on steel products. A shot- or sand-blasted surface is recognized by the fact that it is formed by small circular indentations over the blasted area.

In both operations, a special air spray nozzle is used to propel the round steel shot or sand particles at very high speeds. When these high-speed particles hit the metal surface, they form dents that are proportional to the size and speed of the particle.

Shot blasting of all metals is practical when specified, but sand blasting is somewhat of a problem in the softer metals such as copper, brass, or aluminum.

In soft metals, the sand particles have a tendency to embed in the surface. This can be a serious problem if these particles loosen and fall into such delicate items as bearings or gears in a final assembly.

engine finishing

A highly decorative pattern that is encountered on a less frequent basis is the *engine turned finish*. This finish or pattern is shown in Fig. 9-1.

The engine turned pattern is one formed by grained circles, each overlapping the previous one by some amount. This pattern is produced with the use of a flat-faced hardwood dowel affixed to a drill press and a mixture of oil and emery powder. The workpiece to be finished is located on the work table of the drill press. The hardened flat-faced dowel is secured in the drill chuck and turned at low to medium speeds. As the dowel face is fed down to the plate, a small amount of the oil and emery mixture is placed on the workpiece directly below the dowel face. When

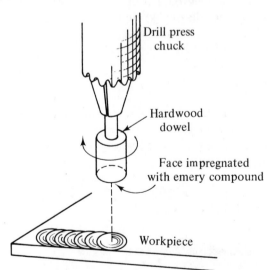

Figure 9-1 — Engine turning.

the dowel makes contact with the work, the emery grits begin to rotate about the center of the dowel. This produces a circular concentric grain pattern. On successive grained circles, each is allowed to overlap the previous one so as to produce a "fish scale" effect.

When one is performing this decorative pattern, a new charge of oil and emery should be used for each circle. This will insure an even grained pattern on the final surface.

[9-3]
painting

Possibly, the most-used surface coating in the sheet metal industry is the painted surface. It is both economical and effective in its decor. In the ferrous or steel product line, it serves well in protecting the metal from rusting or other oxidizing forms.

The two basic forms of painting most used in the general industry are *enamel sprayed surfaces* and the *static-coated surface*. The enamel spray type of surface can be of several forms, air drying, baked, or epoxy base. Each of these is sprayed on by use of an air spray system.

The static-coated surface is unique in that a dry paint powder is sprayed over the electrically charged workpiece. The dry powder, under the influence of the electrical field, evenly coats and adheres to the part. After coating, the workpiece is put into an oven where the powder melts and bonds to the workpiece, forming a smooth, tough surface.

This text will not attempt to explain the many facets of the painting trade, but will rather discuss the preparation of metal prior to painting.

Preparatory to painting, it is most important to inspect the workpiece for scratches, burrs, or weld roughness. These flaws must be corrected prior to painting.

In some instances, surface graining with an orbital sander or hand block is beneficial, especially in areas of high smooth gloss; paint will not bond well to surfaces that are smooth or highly polished. Rust or the initial formation of rust should be removed in all cases encountered. If rust is left on a surface, the paint will adhere to it, not the metal.

Before painting, the surfaces and corners should be cleaned thoroughly of dust, grease, or other foreign material with a solvent or soap and water. If cleaned steel pieces must be stored for some length of time before painting, be sure that they are in a cool dry area that will prevent rusting due to condensation.

[9-4]
electroplating

Electroplating is the process of coating a controlled layer of metal film over the surface of a metal form or part. Plating can be done for decorative purposes or to provide a protective layer against corrosion. The plating process is performed in plating tanks, which use controlled electrical currents to deposit the plating on the part. The base or workpiece metal in most cases is steel, stainless steel, brass, or copper. Aluminum can be plated, but in general it is not finished by this process. Irriditing or anodizing is a more common surface treatment for aluminum.

Accurate control of the current during plating allows the plating thickness to be very accurately controlled. Metals most commonly plated over the surfaces of workpieces are chrome, nickel, copper, and tin. The aforementioned plating metals are ranked in their degree of hardness (chrome being the hardest).

On drawings, plated surfaces are most often defined by *type of plating, surface finish,* and *thickness.*

Surface finishes of plated surfaces fall into three groups: *bright, dull,* or *satin.* Bright plating is mirrorlike in quality, while dull is less reflective. Satin finish plating has no luster and is used extensively on items where glare or gloss would prove a hindrance. Satin chrome-plated measuring scales are a good example; glare could hinder readability.

Plated surfaces in general are less than 0.002 inch thick. Thicker layers may be deposited but only when specified by the print or drawing.

Worn workpieces may be brought up to original size by the process called *precision plating.* This process is often used on round shafting or worn dies to bring them back to their original tolerance. Chrome, being the hardest plating metal, is used exclusively in this resizing operation. Punches, dies, and shear blades resized with chrome plating exhibit very tough, long-lasting working edges.

The electroplating operation is a precise set of steps that begin with the thorough cleaning of the workpiece of all contaminants. Since this process is initiated by the plater, it is not required that the workpiece be cleaned to any great extent. Loose filing, chips, or dust can be removed, but the plater will himself clean the part to his specifications.

[9-5]
anodizing and irriditing

Two processes reserved exclusively for aluminum products are *anodizing* and *irriditing*. Both are used to produce an inert film of aluminum oxide which adheres strongly to the aluminum surface.

Within each of the aforementioned processes, the final layer of aluminum oxide may be dyed (colored). The colors commonly available in anodizing are clear, flat black, clear black, blue, gold, green, and red (copper). Colors other than these mentioned must be compounded by the people performing the process. Irriditing has but two color choices, clear and gold.

Of the two processes, anodizing is the more durable and unique. An anodized surface is extremely hard and resistant to scratching. This is an especially good factor when somewhat soft aluminum sections must be exposed to abrasion. The second feature of an anodized surface is that the layer is an electrical insulator. Most often a good anodized surface will resist voltages up to 500 volts per 0.001-inch depth of anodizing. Irridited surfaces are neither hard nor abrasion resistant, nor are they a good insulator against the flow of electricity.

In general, irridited workpieces are most often specified in the finishes of mechanical or electrical chassis. Anodized surfaces are used for decoration or for areas subject to heavy abrasion, such as control panels, handles, or other exterior surface pieces.

metal preparation

Since in most cases, anodizing is used on decorative or exterior panels, preparation of the workpiece is important. Flaws, scratches, or other surface defects must be grained or emeryed out. Remember, the surface finish of the metal prior to anodizing will be almost identical in nature after anodizing.

Often, in the case of control panels, grained finishes are specified prior to anodizing. These finishes were discussed in a previous section of this chapter.

Irriditing requires little or no preparation, other than removing surface defects. Printed information placed on the metal surface by the manufacturer does not have to be removed, as this is removed during the process.

One final note should be made at this time. Should an aluminum workpiece have fasteners, nuts, springs, or other items not composed of aluminum attached to the workpiece, they must be removed prior to anodizing or irriditing. The influx of metals other than aluminum into either process can and does cause streaking and discoloration of the finished part.

Before we close this chapter, a brief introduction into the steps in these two processes will be given. Its intent is merely to familiarize the reader with the processes used in each treatment.

steps in anodizing and irriditing

Anodizing is performed on aluminum; a series of treating tanks and electrical current is used. The procedural steps in this process are as follows:

Basic Steps in Anodizing

1 / Cleaning

2 / Etching (caustic solution)

3 / Neutralizing

4 / Anodizing (electrical)

5 / Dyeing (not used for clear anodizing)

6 / Sealing

Between each of the steps, starting with step 2, a thorough rinsing is performed before the next operation. This is important so as not to contaminate each tank with chemicals from previous operations.

Irriditing is a relatively simple operation and can be performed without investing a large amount of money or equipment. Solutions and powders necessary for treatment can be purchased at nominal costs. If small metal sections are to be treated, plastic washtubs or buckets can be used. Remember that only two colors are available, clear or gold, and the particular color solution must be procured. The steps in this process are as follows:

Steps in Irriditing

1 / Cleaning

2 / Etching

3 / Neutralizing

4 / Irriditing (clear or gold)

5 / Sealing (optional)

Again, as with anodizing, it is usually recommended that parts be rinsed between steps.

In the etching process, the aluminum part will emerge with a dull grey powdery look. This oxidized film is superficial and is easily rubbed off. Rubbing should be avoided as the mark will show in the final process. If rubs do develop in handling, it is best to remove the entire film with a cloth and re-etch the part.

With the pre-etched piece ready, it can now be immersed in the irriditing bath. Timing in the bath is important for color intensity. Longer immersion gives a deeper gold color. In some instances, the alloy type limits the desired color.

After removal from the irriditing bath, the part is rinsed clean, after which it is put in the sealing bath. Finished parts most often are hung from wire hooks and allowed to air dry.

review questions

9-1 / What are the reasons for finishing a metal surface?

9-2 / Bare finishing of a metal surface is achieved by several methods; list them.

9-3 / Polishing requires what two special items?

9-4 / Define *graining*. What are the two requirements necessary to produce a specified grain finish?

9-5 / Shot or sand blasting techniques make use of what special equipment? Why should tin or copper sheets not be sand blasted?

9-6 / Describe the technique and the tools used to produce an engine turned pattern.

9-7 / Enamel paints are produced in three basic forms. What are they?

9-8 / As a metal technician, what preparation are you required to perform on a workpiece prior to painting?

9-9 / Electroplated surfaces are deposited on metal products for three general purposes; list these reasons.

9-10 / Can aluminum be electroplated?

9-11 / List the basic electro deposited metals most often used. What range of surface finishes can be specified?

9-12 / What is the purpose of precision plating?

9-13 / Anodizing and irriditing are processes used exclusively on what metal?

9-14 / Describe the main features of the anodizing and the irriditing processes.

10

press forming, deep drawing, spinning, and embossing

[10-1]
introduction

Various metal products, circular or odd-shaped in form, are mass produced to meet commercial needs or, in some instances, special applications. A range of such items includes cooking utensils such as cake pans, pots, lids, and pans, and industrial needs such as pressure tanks, float balls, curved sections of automobile bodies, and a host of other items too numerous to list.

Consider items as varied as a coffee pot and an automobile fender with its complex curved geometry. It is a safe assumption that both items were either formed in dies or spun to their final shapes.

The purpose of this chapter is not to teach the practices used in these fields, but rather to list, define, and explain the highlights for a general understanding of the processes. The sheet metal technician will, throughout his career, encounter both die-formed and spun products that will become part of his work project. Knowledge of these methods is also useful in evaluating the methods of mass-producing items in the fastest and least costly way.

[10-2]
press forming

For a simple illustration, let us assume that we are to produce, from flat stock, hemispherical sections with a specified radius. The two hemispheres are later to be bonded together to form a hollow sphere. The most straightforward method of performing this task would be to use a hemispherical metal form over which the flat sheet could be stretched. Obviously, one could not stretch the sheet over the form without creating a wrinkled surface. But what if a male hemispherical form of the proper inner radius were used to press the sheet into a female hemispherical cavity of the proper outer radius? The result would be the formation of a hemisphere of both accurate dimensions and surface smoothness. This, then, is the process of sheet metal pressing or die forming.

In normal operations, metal pressed forms are produced in hydraulic presses, which can in some instances produce pressures exceeding 500 tons per square inch. These high pressures are necessary to deform the sheet metal from its initial form to that defined by the dies. The male formed die is in almost all cases affixed to the movable hydraulic ram of the press. Located accurately with respect to alignment and squareness of the male form, the female die cavity is positioned. The work or press bed with its rugged construction is designed to hold a variety of dies accurately without movement for production of many forms.

An important addition to press metal operations is a device or arrangement called a *pressure plate*. The function of the pressure plate is to locate and clamp the workpiece to the top of the female die block. During forming, the clamp retains the sheet and allows for even forming of the sheet to its final form. After forming, the pressure plate holds the workpiece to the bottom die while the upper die is withdrawn. Finally, the pressure plate is released and the formed section is removed from its die with either an air blast or a mechanical knockout rod located at the bottom of the die. A simple illustration of a press metal die setup is shown in Fig. 10-1.

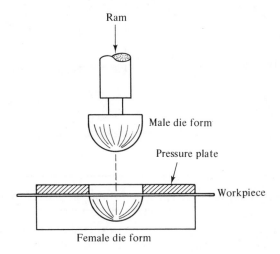

Figure 10-1 — Die forming.

After a metal section has been formed by press dies, the part must go through an operation called *trimming*. The metal that remains under the pressure plate during forming must be removed to produce the final shape of the part. This operation is performed on metal lathes set up to hold and trim the piece, or the piece can be finished by using a slitting machine designed specifically for this operation.

[10-3]
deep drawing

In some designs, single press operations will not produce the desired shape. They will fail because of metal fatigue and subsequent tearing of the sheet stock itself. Long or deep shapes, however, can be formed by a series of forming stages that end with the desired shape. This process of using progressive forming stages is called "deep drawing." The process is expensive from two standpoints: cost of the dies required to form the product, and the time involved in performing the operations. The steps required in forming a typical deep section are illustrated in Fig. 10-2.

Press or deep drawing operations can be performed on a variety of sheet metal products in the cold state. Some materials during forming, however, become "work hardened" and brittle. If further forming is required, the piece often must be annealed. When the metal is in the

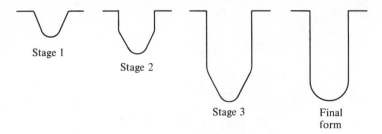

Figure 10-2 — Deep drawing by stages.

annealed or soft temper state, further forming is possible without fear of tearing the workpiece.

Heavy plates of steel, copper, stainless steel, or other metals can be press formed but often must be in a heated plastic state. This allows the plate to be formed easily without undue pressure requirements on the press and without fracturing of the metal form itself.

[10-4]
spinning

In Section 10-2, we introduced the theory of press forming metal parts with the idea of stretching the sheet metal over a male form of the desired shape. It was further stated that this was not feasible, and the female cavity die was introduced. However, with the process called *spinning,* we can indeed stretch the metal sheet over a male form without use of a female cavity.

This process can be used on a wide range of metal thicknesses. As with press forming, the metal may be worked in the cold or heated plastic state. Simple and complex pieces can be formed with this process. Figure 10-3 illustrates some of the more simple shapes produced by spinning.

basics of spinning

The basic requirement in spinning is that the circular flat sheet to be worked be located firmly between the male form and an adjustable center bearing ram. The male form with the clamped sheet is then rotated together, with the bearing ram providing the necessary clamping pressure. Most often, this operation is performed on a standard engine lathe or a specially constructed one called a *spinning lathe*.

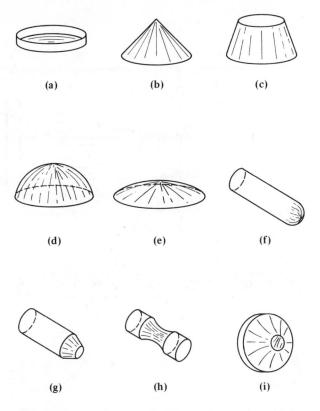

(a) (b) (c)

(d) (e) (f)

(g) (h) (i)

Figure 10-3 — Some typical shapes formed by spinning.

Thin, soft-gauge metals such as aluminum, brass, copper, and silver can often be shaped over male forms made of hardwood such as oak or maple. Thicker or tougher metal sections require metal forms made of steel or, if small in size, hard brass.

Two tools are used to operate on and form the metal sheet over the form: the *forming bar* and the *backing bar*. These tools are designed to be held and controlled with hand pressure. The more sophisticated tools are equipped with hardened roller bearing work ends, but they can be as simple as two hardwood dowels with tapered and radiused tips. Wooden tools are, however, limited to working thin-gauge soft metals such as copper, silver, gold, and soft brass. Figure 10-4 shows a typical spinning setup with the forming and backing bars in contact with the workpiece.

The forming and backing bars are both rested and pivoted on a support bar of steel which has a series of holes located along its length. The pins used to pivot the tools can be removed and replaced at various hole locations to effect good tool-to-work-sheet contact.

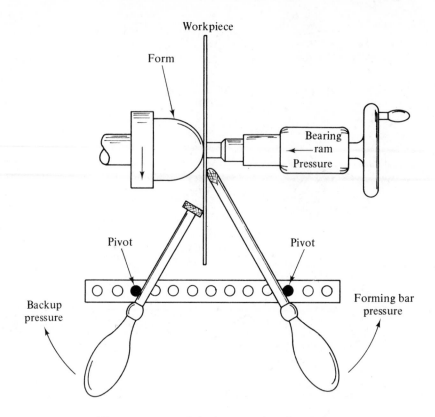

Figure 10-4 — Spinning technique in a lathe.

In practice, the backing tool is located and pivoted so as to contact and support the back surface of the rotating work sheet. The forming tool is positioned and pivoted so that firm contact near the center of the workpiece is made. With firm pressure and small sweeping arcs away from the sheet center, the forming tool begins the process. Backup pressure near the forming tool is important at all times during forming tool contact. The backing tool provides two necessary functions: It provides back support so that forming tool pressure can effectively stretch the metal between it and the center clamping ram. It also prevents the sheet from developing radial ripples around its unformed surface. The backup tool should, in every case, be placed closer to the forming tool for better control of the operation. The arrangement of the backup and forming tools is shown in Fig. 10-4.

During the spinning of certain metals, such as copper or silver, a tendency to work harden is often encountered before the piece is finished. One or several annealing operations are often employed on the workpiece.

After each annealing, the part is reinstalled on the form and further spinning is performed.

When the final shape is achieved, the metal may be grained or polished while still in the lathe. Excess metal is also removed or trimmed from the formed piece prior to its removal.

Thicker formed sections, such as large storage tank ends or pressure heads, are shaped over metal forms in a heated plastic state. Heavy steel rollers are employed to force the heated flat stock to its final form. The rollers in this case are controlled by powered screws while preshaped templates control the path taken by the roller.

In summary, many complex shapes are produced by the process of spinning or rolling. The more complex shapes may employ the use of several intermediate forms or breakapart forms. Breakapart forms are those that have individual sections fastened together to produce a desired shape. After forming, the sections are unfastened and removed from the finished part.

[10-5]
embossing

The process called embossing is a very old practice in the sheet metal trades. In fact, this process has been employed by man for thousands of years in producing artistic metal forms. In general terms, embossing is the process whereby simple tools or preshaped tools are used to displace and cause a recessed or raised area to be formed in a workpiece. The displaced shape can be produced by striking the embossing tool or, as in industrial processes, it may be machine formed, with two-part embossing rolls being used.

This process differs from engraving because no material is removed to produce the final result.

A common practice in both the machine and sheet metal trades is the *stenciling* of names, numbers, or other information on metal bars or sheets. (Stenciling is in reality an embossing operation.) This information is used to identify or to put serial numbers on parts of major assemblies. Parts that are to be stenciled are specified on the drawing, which gives the required wording or numbers as well as the height in which the information is to appear. Commercial stencils are made in both letter and number sets. Symbol heights are made in $\frac{1}{8}$-, $\frac{5}{32}$-, $\frac{3}{16}$-, and $\frac{1}{4}$-inch sizes.

Stencil sets are made in both hand-held and machine-held sizes. The symbols are positive or male in form and are made of hardened tool steel.

Use of the hand stencil requires that each letter or number be selected individually. The hand stencil is aligned to some edge or line and given a sharp impact from a hammer. The stencil is then removed, and the indentation in the metal is inspected. If the indentation is not fully formed, the stencil is reinserted and allowed to align with the indentation. A second or third hit with the hammer is then used to form the symbol evenly in the metal.

For repetitive stenciling, the word, numbers, or combinations can be placed in a holder and individually secured. This holder can then be placed in a press brake or punch press and set to produce any number of stencils or embossings.

Embossed sheet metal products are commercially produced to answer the needs of both decorative and practical applications. Three basic patterns used extensively are the *random-irregular,* the *diamond,* and the *corrugated.* These patterns are shown in Fig. 10-5.

The *random-irregular pattern* is used exclusively on thin-gauge aluminum sheeting. This pattern is used on small appliances, barbeque grills, or decorative panels.

The *diamond embossed* pattern is produced in both thin-gauge aluminum and thin-to-medium-gauge steel. Although its design can be used for decorative purposes, its major use is in metal flooring. The diamond pattern is excellent for this application, since it affords a safe, nonslip surface on which to walk.

The final pattern which can be considered embossed is the *corrugated pattern.* This design is of special importance in the roofing and drainage fields, since it increases the strength of the original flat metal sheet with its "corrugated" raised ribs.

Embossing of sheet stock is efficiently and economically performed by using embossing rolls (Fig. 10-6). These rolls are made so that the forms or shapes are produced on the rolls themselves in a male-female design pattern. When sheet stock is passed through such a roll setup, the male pattern presses the material into the female cavity. This produces the embossed design.

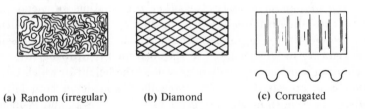

(a) Random (irregular)   (b) Diamond   (c) Corrugated

Figure 10-5 — Embossed sheet metal types.

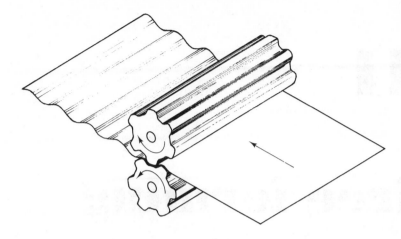

Figure 10-6 — Embossing rolls for corrugation.

review questions

10-1 / Describe the basic operation of press forming.

10-2 / What is the purpose of the pressure plate in press forming?

10-3 / How does deep drawing differ from press forming?

10-4 / What dictates a single or progressive forming of a workpiece?

10-5 / Define the operation of *spinning*.

10-6 / What two tools are used to shape the metal sheet in spinning?

10-7 / At the beginning of the spinning process, where are the forming tools located? How are they held in the machine?

10-8 / On complex spun sections, multi-piece forms are often used. What are they called?

10-9 / Define *embossing* and *stenciling*.

10-10 / Commercial sheet are made with what three basic forms of embossing?

11

free forming

[11-1]
free formed pieces

Since man's first discovery of metal, he has shaped and formed it into a wide range of objects from weapons to works of art. In most cases, these shapes were hand formed, the simplest of tools being used. This process of hand forming metal with basic tools is called *free forming*.

This chapter is included for a single purpose. That purpose is to offer to the artistic reader the basic forms, methods, and processes used by previous metalsmiths to create metal art forms. Art creations will be shown within the chapter with no real dimensions given.

Artistically inclined students should use their own talents in producing shapes, patterns, and art forms. Remember, you possess the knowledge of both hand tools and metal. The only ingredient now required is creativity and some basic techniques.

[11-2]
hammer forming (introduction)

Hammer forming of metal into special forms is possibly the most basic process used. The artisans of years ago were forced in many cases to produce a metal section of required thickness by beating a larger one to the necessary thickness. This process in most cases was done by heating the metal to a red-hot plastic state and striking it with a hammer. The blacksmith, even in today's world, fashions and sizes a horseshoe by using this simple process.

[11-3]
wrought iron effect

A wrought iron effect, often used to produce decorative surfaces, is formed by the impact of a hammer on the flat surface of a metal piece. Door hinges, straps, or lock assemblies are often given this special effect.

In essence, the smooth surface of a workpiece is dimpled over its entire surface with the ball end of the ball peen hammer. The dimples are circular in shape and vary in depth and diameter. These variations in size are achieved by altering the impact force of the hammer on the metal surface. For a true wrought surface appearance, the dimples should be random in placement and size. They should be formed so that they tend to leave very little of the original flat metal surface remaining. A typical wrought iron peened surface is shown in Fig. 11-1.

The wrought iron effect can be formed on any metal of a soft to medium temper. Steel, aluminum, copper, and brass are excellent choices for producing this effect. To enhance the final appearance, a flat black paint can be sprayed or brushed over the surface.

A very attractive surface is obtained on copper and brass by merely buffing the raised surfaces about the depressions and not allowing the buffing wheel to penetrate into the dimples. This contrasted surface of

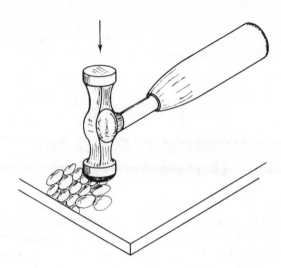

Figure 11-1 — Wrought iron effect by peening.

polished and dull sections can be protected from tarnishing or dulling by a protective coating of lacquer. Further to enhance a dimpled brass or copper piece, a process of back filling the depressions is performed. Usually a flat black paint is spread over the surface. Before it dries, the surface is wiped clean with a rag. The raised areas are free of paint, while pools remain in the depressions. A light buffing on the outer surface enhances the contrast.

A simple but attractive project that incorporates a wrought iron pattern with a stenciled legend is shown in Fig. 11-2. This piece, made of sheet stock steel, brass or aluminum, can be expanded to become a belt buckle, a bracelet, or a nameplate for a desk or brandy bottle. The main form with its bordered wrought iron effect can be developed by two methods. The undimpled area can be protected during hammering with a cover plate, or the stenciled plate can be sweat soldered over the main piece after dimpling. The soldered overlay may be of similar or different metal.

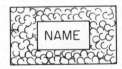

Figure 11-2 — Peened and stenciled form.

[11-4]
hammer or
beaten forms

A variety of artistic or prototype forms can be and often are beaten into shape with hammer blows with a solid backing surface being used. Both soft- and hard-faced hammers may be used. The process of beating has a forming and stretching effect on the metal being hammered.

Backing surfaces, used to support and form the sheet metal section, can exist in three basic forms: a *flat surface*, a *female-formed cavity*, and a *shot bag* (Fig. 11-3). The one common characteristic that they possess is that they do not mar or scratch the metal being shaped. The most simple backing surface is a solid block of hardwood, such as a section of tree trunk. Cut to a convenient height, it serves as an inexpensive but solid backing surface.

If more than one hand-beaten form is to be produced, a hardwood block with the required shape carved or machined into it is the best approach. The flat sheet, prior to forming, can be wood-screwed around the edge of the cavity. This will secure and retain the sheet during its deformation.

The leather or canvas shot bag is an aid used by only the most experienced sheet metal technician. Its main use is in producing special depressions or raised portions on a finished sheet or form section. Some examples of shot bag formings are illustrated in Fig. 11-4.

Not all metals lend themselves to hammer forming. A good selection should have characteristics of being highly malleable and in a soft temper

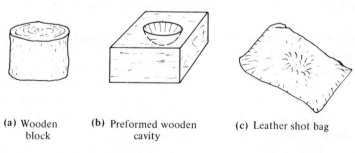

| (a) Wooden block | (b) Preformed wooden cavity | (c) Leather shot bag |

Figure 11-3 — Hammer forming aids.

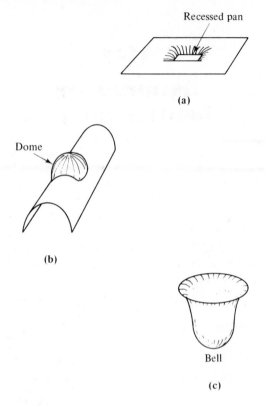

Recessed pan

(a)

Dome

(b)

Bell

(c)

Figure 11-4 — Examples of shot bag forming.

state. Materials that lend themselves well to this process are gold, silver, lead, copper, soft brasses, and aluminum.

During various stages of hammer forming, copper and brass sheet stock begin to change to a spring temper state. This change is called "work hardening." Further hammer forming proves difficult, and in some instances the metal stock tears or splits.

Annealing operations may have to be performed at various stages until the final form is obtained. Copper is annealed quite easily by heating it to a red glow and immediately quenching it in cold water. Brass annealing is best performed by allowing the heated material to cool to room temperature at a very slow rate. Do not attempt to hasten the process by air movement or water cooling. The annealing process stated for copper works equally well with silver or aluminum.

An excellent material for beginners or highly advanced artists is copper. Copper works well in forming simple or complex shapes. The finished piece can then be buffed to a highly polished state and sprayed with a protective coating of lacquer.

The first encounters with hammer forming should be small in size and of simple design. A shape in the form of a bowl would be a good first attempt. A circular disc of soft copper about 6 to 8 inches in diameter with a thickness between 0.031 and 0.062 inch will produce a good-sized bowl.

For this project, a 4 by 4-inch block of hard wood can be used as the backing surface. The end grain of the block should be used as the actual backing surface. This is important to keep the block from splintering from the hammer blows.

basic steps

Prior preparation of the backing block is most important before forming. A shallow circular depression is formed with the ball end of the ball peen hammer. This forms an area where metal from the flat sheet form is depressed from a hammer hit. As one's skills increase, dimpled depressions of various diameters and depth may exist on the block face. The various-sized dimples have the effect of producing large or small curves to a workpiece as it is being formed.

The beginning strikes with the hammer must begin around the outer edge of the disc. This pattern is produced around the edge, forming a concentric ring. During this initial beating, the flat sheet, held in the hand, has its edge opposite the forming pocket raised or lowered. Raising the side opposite the forming area controls the amount of flare or radius of the hammered edge.

A series of concentric hammered rings is now produced along the same lines as discussed above. Each new ring is smaller in diameter than its neighbor. If the bowl has a flat bottom, the hammer forming terminates at its boundary. This boundary would have been scribed on the flat sheet prior to forming. The hammering process is repeated, beginning with the outer edge, until the desired form is achieved. It is during these repeated hammering processes that the desired shape is approached. Holding the form at various work angles for each ring formation directs the form and shape of that section. This is illustrated in Fig. 11-5.

In the final finishing stages, small irregularities between the formed rings are blended with a small hammer and light blows.

Before passing to our next section, one final thought must be given. Hammer forming is a slow, painstaking process. Do not attempt to speed the process by overforming with the hammer. The real mark of a fine workpiece is the time and patience that went into its creation.

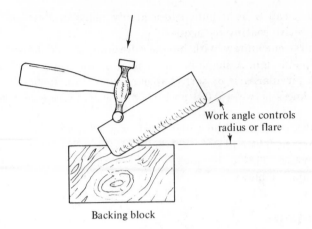

Work angle controls
radius or flare

Backing block

Figure 11-5

[11-5]
embossing techniques

Embossing, as previously described, is the process of producing raised or depressed shapes in a material with no material removal involved. These depressions, produced by formed punches, may be letters, numbers, lines, circles, or any number of shapes.

This art form, like hammer forming, has been in existence since man began working metal into useful products.

The basic principle of embossing is that of using a tool harder than the workpiece to produce the desired effect. The tool when struck with a hammer causes the metal of the workpiece to displace and reproduce the shape of the punch face. Embossing can be performed on a wide range of metal shapes that include flat stock, round bar, cylinders, or special shapes. In cases where the material is both thin and of a soft nature, a backing plate of lead, copper, or hardwood must be used. These materials, due to their softness, allow good depth to embossing punches without the material's being punctured. The depth of the embossed figure is also controlled by the force of the hammer blow.

Tools for artistic embossing are for the most part made from old or reground tool steel punches. A good basic starter set should include several punches ground with hemispherical ends of various diameters, a chisel with a ¼- to ⁵⁄₁₆-inch width, and a center punch. This starter set of tools will allow a wide range of embossed patterns, straight lines, and geometric shapes that will fill most needs.

The basic step leading to embossing is in the development of a pattern or design. Very often, this is done on a piece of paper with the normal tools for pencil drawings. A paper layout is also the best and most accurate method of transferring the design to the workpiece. The method is especially suited for use on round or curved surfaces. The paper, with its pattern, is glued or taped directly to the surface.

Prior to tool contact, some thought should be given to the shape and styles that will be used on borders, lines, and other areas of embossing. Once a pattern has been produced, it cannot be flattened and redone.

Art work other than patterns can be produced with the embossing process. An illustrative embossed scene is shown in Fig. 11-6.

[11-6]
embossing scenes

Scene embossing is most often performed on a flat copper sheet having a soft-to-medium-hard wood backing attached to it. The scene may be drawn directly on the sheet with a scriber, or a paper overlay containing the design may be glued to the copper surface.

Two methods of producing the embossed scene are available: *hollow relief* and *bas-relief*.

Hollow relief is the process of forming the main character or figure in the scene in a recessed depression. Lesser forms are also recessed but not as deeply as the main figure.

Bas-relief is the process of forming a scene in which the main forms

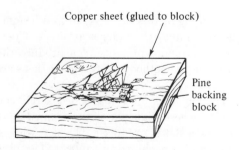

Copper sheet (glued to block)

Pine backing block

Figure 11-6 — Embossed scene.

seem to project outward from the background. Lesser forms also project, but they are not as pronounced as the main form.

To produce our scene, shown in Fig. 11-6, in hollow relief, we would proceed with the following steps. The area of the sky is embossed back slightly from the water area. The ship figure, the main character, is now worked to some depth with respect to the ''recessed'' sky area.

The clouds can now be embossed at a depth much less than that of the main form. Curved and rounded surfaces within the form of the ship and clouds are produced so as to give a three-dimensional effect. The remaining scene lines, the waves, are embossed slightly below the surface plane of the water.

Development of a bas-relief, in some instances, can be produced with the hollow relief technique. This is to say that a hollow relief formed in thin material will, when turned over, produce a bas-relief of somewhat less clarity in form. The very nature of embossing tools and their design make the process of direct bas-relief forming extremely difficult.

[11-7]
combined free forms

Most of the metal art forms created for both display or sale are combinations of basic shapes that are fastened together by soldering, welding, or other methods. The purpose of this section is to combine these processes and methods with creativity to produce attractive metal sculpture and art forms.

A simple but attractive form used throughout the world in many designs is the scroll form. This form and variations can be produced quite easily with thin-gauge rectangular strips of hot rolled steel, aluminum, or brass.

Commercial forming of this shape is done on benders that have been set up to produce large numbers of identical pieces. The metal craftsman, using simple tooling and hand pressure, can produce these scroll forms. Scroll forms and a simple method of producing them are shown in Fig. 11-7.

Either a single-ended or a double-ended scroll can be formed by using a piece of pipe whose diameter is determined by the scroll's size. In one end of the pipe a slot is produced. The slot, wide enough to accept the stock thickness, can be machined or saw cut. The pipe with its slot is now clamped in a bench vise.

Before continuing with our scroll forming, let us look at its design

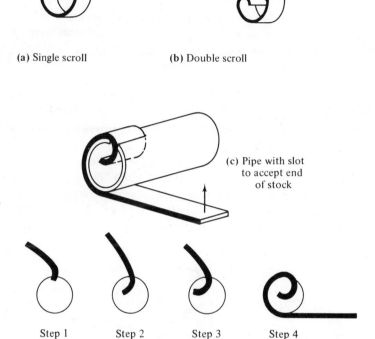

(a) Single scroll   (b) Double scroll

(c) Pipe with slot
to accept end
of stock

Step 1   Step 2   Step 3   Step 4

Figure 11-7 — Scroll forming with pipe.

more closely. A well-formed scroll is in the form of a spiral. The inner
section appears to decrease in radius as it approaches the imaginary
center of the shape. It is this inner section of the scroll that must be
preshaped before the larger outer bend is produced.

This preforming of the inner section is shown in three end-view
steps in Fig. 11-7. In the first step, a small amount of the flat stock is
inserted into the pipe slot. A small bend is produced. The second step
requires that a small amount more of the flat stock be inserted into the
pipe and given another bend. The third step approximates the tight inner
curve of the scroll. Once its form is satisfactory, the final large bend is
produced by hand forming about the pipe. After completion, the finished
scroll is slid out of the pipe slot. The other end of the strip can, if required, be scrolled with the same approach as listed above.

Often a wrought hammer finish on the scroll stock gives an excellent appearance. Remember to produce this or other selected surface finishes prior to forming.

Unique and spectacular designs can be produced by combining scrolled forms. They can be secured by either riveting, welding, or bolting.

Metal sculpture is often used to depict the various life forms, be they animal or plant. The sculpture may also be representative of inanimate objects, such as windmills, bridges, ships, or others. These creations are most often made of thin-gauge soft metals, such as copper or brass. They can be and are also made of saw- or flame-cut steel, welded into some final form.

To show some of the basic techniques of metal sculpturing, let us look at the metal flowers shown in Fig. 11-8. Here are two flowers, a daisy and a tulip. When sculpting a shape, try to break its composition into simple parts that may be produced with simple methods. Looking at our daisy blossom, we can see that it contains a center disk with eight petals located around its shape. To attempt a serious reproduction of its form, we should start with its center disk. In true form, it is a concave or spherical disk. This section could be formed from a circular flat piece of

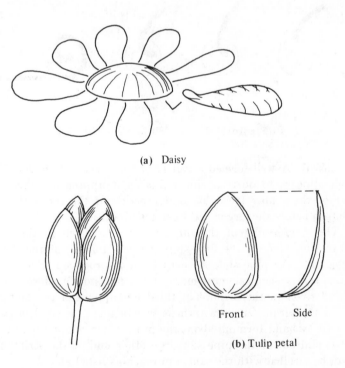

(a) Daisy

Front   Side

(b) Tulip petal

Figure 11-8 — Metal sculpturing.

copper or brass by using the technique of hammer forming previously discussed. If the disk is of a small size, it is better to form this shape on a large flat sheet with a dimpled backing block being used. The finished disk can then be cut from the flat sheet. The petals can be laid out from a template and hand-sheared from the flat sheet.

As shown in Fig. 11-8, a small tail is formed on the petal. The tail's purpose is to serve as a solder connection to the blossom disk at its final assembly. Forming and contouring each petal can be done by using a hammer and a dimple-shaped cavity in the backing block. If very thin soft metal is used, finger forming is possible. The outer tips of the petals can be pressed over a steel ball from an old bearing.

The final assembly of the blossom is best achieved by soldering. The center disk, placed face down, is pretinned, as are the tails of each petal. The final soldering of each petal is now performed.

A stem for our blossom can be of heavy gauge copper or brass wire. The "stem" wire is soldered to the underside of the center disk. Leaves, formed of thin copper, are cut, formed, or embossed, and attached to the main stem and blossom.

The tulip in the lower half of our figure uses four sides, as depicted. After the four petals are formed, they are assembled at their overlapping bases with solder. Stems and leaves can be assembled as described above.

[11-8]
summary

This chapter was a basic introduction to the more simple techniques of artistic metal forming. Those readers who find this form to their liking will surely develop and improve what has been discussed.

Since free forming is such an old art, the tools are both simple and inexpensive. Where tools are not available, the avid artisan will fashion and create them to his personal needs. Again, as a final reminder, the work is tedious and slow, and the quality of the finished piece will reflect the time spent on it.

review questions

11-1 / When metal is hand formed using basic tools and techniques, what is it called?

11-2 / Describe a wrought iron effect and how it is achieved.

11-3 / To enhance a wrought iron effect on metal, the dimples can be backfilled with what?

11-4 / Hand hammer forming of metal pieces is achieved using what three basic surfaces?

11-5 / When using a female form to produce a desired shape, the metal sheet is secured by what means?

11-6 / Describe what is done to anneal a copper workpiece that has work hardened.

11-7 / Artistic pieces can be embossed in two forms. List them and describe their specific differences.

11-8 / When producing a scroll form, what steps are necessary to produce a good result?

11-9 / Producing metal sculpture requires that the chosen form be subdivided according to what criteria?

11-10 / List some common metals that lend themselves to cold hammer forming.

11-11 / Two methods of scene layout on a workpiece are used. What are these methods?

11-12 / A basic set of embossing tools can be made from what items?

11-13 / Artistic metal creations require what two main ingredients?

12

project section

The projects discussed in this section were selected to summarize most of the important facets of basic sheet metal operations.

It is recommended in student-teacher groups that the student work closely with his instructor. His knowledge and past experience are invaluable to your understanding and growth in this field. No one book can replace the personal attention and aid that an experienced instructor has to offer.

To those readers who have embarked on a self-teaching program, be sure to ask those people in the trades questions that you may have about machinery at your disposal.

[lesson 1]
paper construction,
layout, stretchouts

Using paper, pencil, ruler, compass, and a protractor, perform the constructions listed below.

1-1 / Figure 12-1 shows a piece of paper 8½ by 11 inches. A rectangle 4 by 6½ inches is located within this sheet as shown. Using parallel line and perpendicular construction methods, locate the required rectangle. Leave all construction lines used to produce the rectangle.

1-2 / The following is noted on a print: "8 holes ½ inch dia through, located equally on a 6.250 D.B.C." Lay out the location of these holes. What is the length of chord between two successive holes?

1-3 / Using paper, construct a right circular cone with a base diameter of 3 inches and a slant height (s) of 5 inches.

1-4 / Lay out and form on paper a frustum of a right cone whose large base is 2 inches in diameter with a small upper base of 1-inch diameter. The slant height of this frustum is 1¾ inches. Form this frustum, using the radial line method.

1-5 / Figure 12-2 shows a dimensioned hexagonal pyramid shape. Develop the true shape of one face and then produce the full pattern to produce the figure.

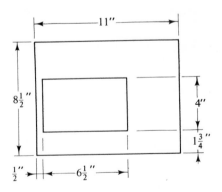

Figure 12-1

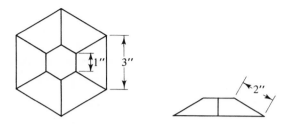

Figure 12-2

1-6 / Calculate and lay out the following intervals or even spaces:

a. Five spaces in a 7.375-inch length.

b. Five spaces over a 15-inch length.

c. Ten spaces over a 12-inch length.

d. Twenty-seven spaces in a 13-inch length.

1-7 / Figure 12-3 shows three forms, each made of $\frac{1}{16}$-inch C.R.S. material. Calculate the stretchout for each form.

1-8 / Using Problem 1-7, lay out on paper the flat pattern of each form. Shade the bend allowance for each bend.

1-9 Locate the center of the $3\frac{7}{16}$-inch side shown in Fig. 12-3(c). Locate the center from each end of the stretchout.

1-10 / Using Fig. 4-2 in Chapter 4, calculate the rectangular sheet that the stretchout will fit on.

[lesson 2]
hand tool creations
in sheet metal

Tools — Scale, bevel, protractor, scriber, divider, centerpunch, hammer, hand shears.

Material — Thin-gauge soft aluminum, tin-plated steel or galvanized steel (about 0.020 inch thick).

Project — Figure 12-4 shows three geometric shapes that are to be laid out on flat sheet stock to within $\frac{1}{64}$ inch of their given sizes.

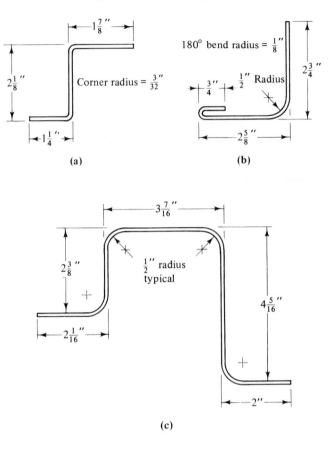

Figure 12-3

Both (a) and (b) of Fig. 12-4 can be produced by using geometric constructions or a square head and scale. Be sure to check that the dimensions of the layouts are within a tolerance of $\pm\frac{1}{64}$ inch of the given sizes.

The circle shown in Fig. 12-4 is produced with a diameter equal to $3\frac{13}{16}$ inch. Using this diameter and Table 4-1, space off 12 equal spaces about the circumference. Connect these points to the center of the circle with straight lines. On each line connecting the spacing with the center of the circle, stencil numbers from 0 to 11 as shown.

Using the regular pattern and curved-blade hand shears, cut the shapes from the flat stock. Lightly file any burrs that exist on the sheared edges and flatten the shapes by light strikes from a soft-faced hammer against a flat metal surface.

These three metal forms are in actuality tools that can be used in

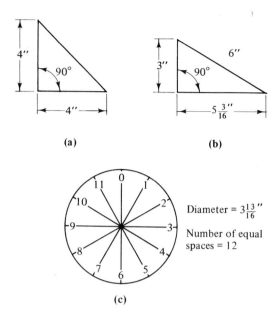

Figure 12-4

work practices. The two triangles are basic to both the metal and drawing trades, as Fig. 12-4(a) is a 45°-45°-90° triangle, while Fig. 12-4(b) is a 30°-60°-90° triangle.

The circle with its 12 numbered divisions has a circumference equal to 12 inches. This makes each division equal to 1 inch. This tool can be used by initially aligning the zero number line with a starting or reference point. By counting the number of revolutions or spaces used in reaching a distance from the starting point, the length in inches or feet and inches can be determined. If one produced 48 equal spaces about this circumference, each increment would have a value of $\frac{1}{4}$ inch.

[lesson 3]
orthographic drawing, chord and spacing calculations

3-1 / Figure 12-5 shows a solid form with dimensions. On an $8\frac{1}{2}$ by 11-inch piece of paper, draw its top, front, right side, left side, back, and bottom views. (Note that the top and front views are noted).

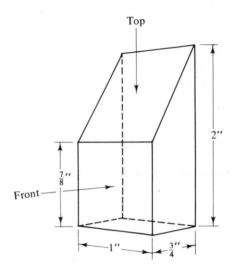

Figure 12-5

3-2 / If you were given a print of a sheet metal fabrication and were asked to produce the part, what specific items would you seek out on the print prior to starting the workpiece?

3-3 / Refer to Fig. 4-2. Calculate and produce the stretchout for the part in thin cardboard. Fold the stretchout to its final form. (Assume the cardboard to be $\frac{1}{16}$ inch thick.)

3-4 / Calculate the chordal constant for each of the given bolt circle patterns. Using a pencil compass, produce the layouts on paper.

a / Five spaces on a 3-inch D.B.C.

b / Twelve spaces on a 4¾-inch D.B.C.

c / Six spaces on a 5⅝-inch D.B.C.

d / Eight spaces on a 2-inch-radius bolt circle

3-5 / Figure 12-6 shows a flat section to be laid out. The tolerance of the dimensions is $\pm\frac{1}{32}$ inch. As noted, there are 5 holes equally spaced over a length of 4 inches. Produce this layout on paper within the specified tolerance.

3-6 / Using available sheet metal scraps or samples, determine their thicknesses, using a 0- to 1-inch micrometer. Tabulate the various thicknesses of at least six pieces. Using the table included in this text, select gauge sizes that most closely match the size of each. Next to each selected gauge size, record the micrometer reading obtained from that specific sheet.

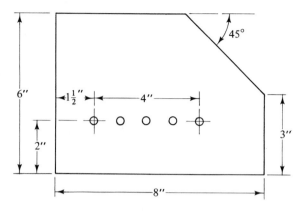

Figure 12-6

3-7 / Suppose that you were given a metric-dimensioned print that showed a rectangular sheet 28.5 cm long by 13.8 cm wide by 2.5 mm thick. Calculate the above length and width of the sheet with English dimensions. Select a gauge of sheet that is closest to 2.5 mm thick without exceeding the thickness.

[lesson 4]
truncated hexagonal
metal tray

4-1 / List the basic parts of the hand-operated shear.

4-2 / What two items are important in sizing a shear?

4-3 / What is the main purpose of having the top shear blade at an angle to the bottom blade?

4-4 / List three items on a hand shear that are useful in forming shapes and sizes of specified workpieces.

4-5 / Figure 12-7 shows various shapes made from flat sheet. List those that you feel could not be produced if only a hand-operated shear is used.

4-6 / Figure 12-8 shows a truncated hexagonal shape that would appear on a drawing. Using its given dimensions, develop a true-size face and produce a layout. The final formed section is to have soft soldered seams. Select either brass, copper, or tin-plated steel with

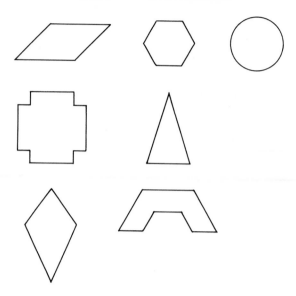

Figure 12-7

a thickness range between 0.020 to 0.032 inch for the workpiece. The use of the hand shear, tinsnips, and leaf brake is required for this project. The final form can be used for several useful items; a candle holder, an ash tray, or a base for a statue or other work of art.

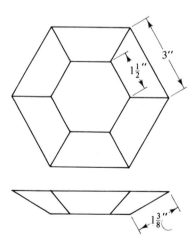

Figure 12-8

[lesson 5]
flange-out box
and slide lid

Figure 12-9 shows a simple box and lid as would be depicted on a drawing. Develop the stretchout lengths and widths of the box and the lid in the required materials. Using the hand shear, hand notcher, and leaf or press brake, produce the final shapes. Solder, with 60—40 (lead—tin) solder, all corner seams for rigidity.

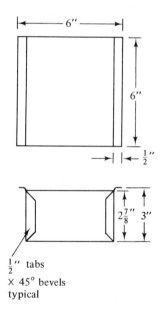

$\frac{1}{2}''$ tabs
✕ 45° bevels
typical

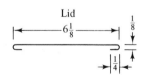

Lid

Material: 0.032 C.R. steel
Tolerance: ± $\frac{1}{32}''$

Figure 12-9

[lesson 6]
square section
canister with
top and bottom

Figure 12-10 shows a canister with its body and end covers detailed. Material to produce this form should be solderable (C.R. steel, brass, or copper). The final form can be used as a tobacco or salt canister. Note that if the form is made of copper or brass, its interior surfaces should be lined or painted to prevent contact with food.

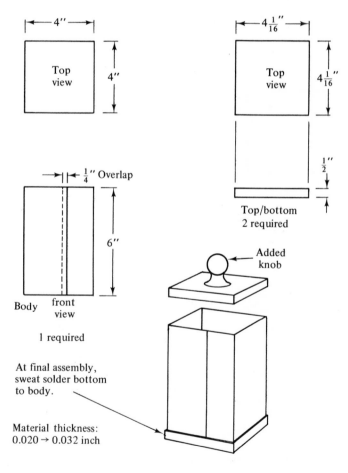

Figure 12-10

[lesson 7]
taper front-
and back-sided pan

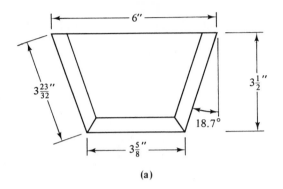

(a)

Notes:

1. $\frac{1}{2}$″ tabs on ends only.
2. Lead-tin solder tabs to ends for watertight seal.

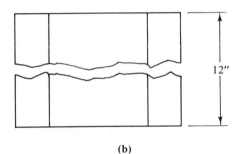

(b)

Taper-sided pan

Material: 0.020- or 0.025-inch tinned steel

Tolerance: $\pm\frac{1}{16}$″

Bend radii: $\frac{1}{16}$″

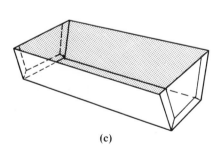

(c)

[lesson 8]
sheet metal joints
(formed)

Shear, from C.R. steel sheet of about 0.020 to 0.035 inch thick, pieces with dimensions of 3" × 6" ($\pm\frac{1}{64}$").

Using these sheared pieces, produce the following seams. Produce the seams along the 3" width.

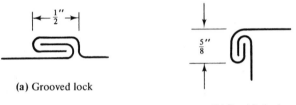

(a) Grooved lock

(b) Double lock

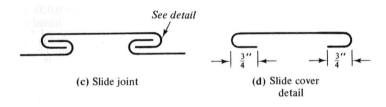

(c) Slide joint

See detail

(d) Slide cover detail

[lesson 9]
drinking mug

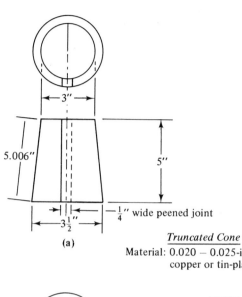

3″

5.006″

5″

3½″

—¼″ wide peened joint

(a)

Truncated Cone
Material: 0.020 − 0.025-inch thick
copper or tin-plated steel

3½″ diameter
disk x 0.035
thick tin-plated
steel or copper

Base
(b)

9″

⅛″ wide
hems

3″⁄8

both edges

(c)

Free form
handle
(hems in)

(d)

Handle
Material: Tin-plated steel or copper
0.020 − 0.025-inch thick

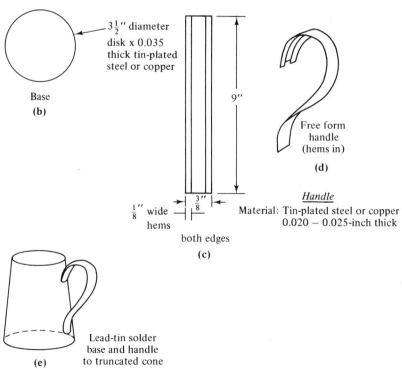

Lead-tin solder
base and handle
to truncated cone

(e)

[lesson 10]
flange-in box
with hinged cover

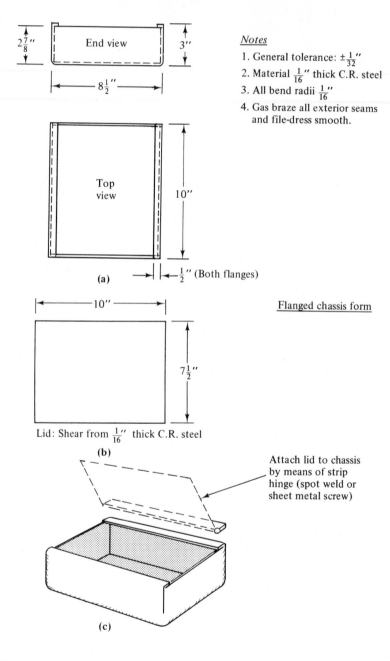

End view

$2\frac{7}{8}''$

$3''$

$8\frac{1}{2}''$

Notes
1. General tolerance: $\pm\frac{1}{32}''$
2. Material $\frac{1}{16}''$ thick C.R. steel
3. All bend radii $\frac{1}{16}''$
4. Gas braze all exterior seams and file-dress smooth.

Top view

$10''$

(a)

$\frac{1}{2}''$ (Both flanges)

Flanged chassis form

$10''$

$7\frac{1}{2}''$

Lid: Shear from $\frac{1}{16}''$ thick C.R. steel

(b)

Attach lid to chassis by means of strip hinge (spot weld or sheet metal screw)

(c)

[lesson 11]
folding chair

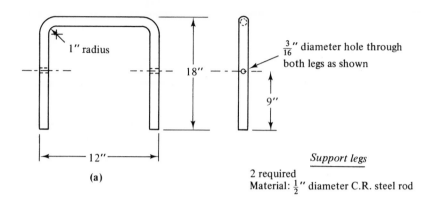

1" radius

18"

9"

$\frac{3}{16}$" diameter hole through both legs as shown

12"

(a)

Support legs

2 required
Material: $\frac{1}{2}$" diameter C.R. steel rod

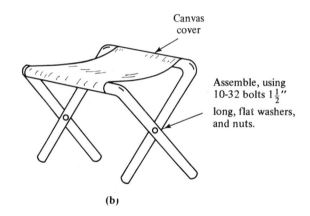

Canvas cover

Assemble, using 10-32 bolts $1\frac{1}{2}$"

long, flat washers, and nuts.

(b)

[lesson 12]
book shelf

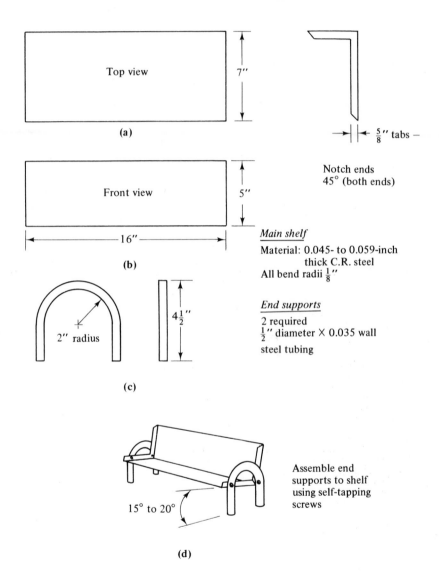

Top view

7″

(a)

Front view

5″

|← 16″ →|

(b)

2″ radius

4½″

(c)

⅝″ tabs —

Notch ends
45° (both ends)

Main shelf

Material: 0.045- to 0.059-inch
thick C.R. steel
All bend radii ⅛″

End supports

2 required
½″ diameter × 0.035 wall
steel tubing

15° to 20°

Assemble end
supports to shelf
using self-tapping
screws

(d)

[lesson 13]
magazine holder

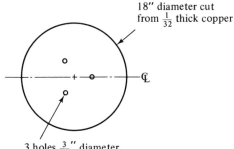

18" diameter cut
from $\frac{1}{32}$ thick copper

3 holes $\frac{3}{16}$ " diameter
equally spaced on a
6" D.B.C.

Base

(a)

Notes

1. After cutting to size
and placing required
holes, ball peen finish
all over.

2. Roll disk about indicated
center line to a curved
section with a 9" radius.

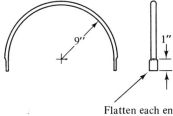

9"

1"

Flatten each end
of hoop in vise

(b)

Hoop handle
$\frac{1}{2}$ " diameter x 0.020 wall
brass tubing x 31" long

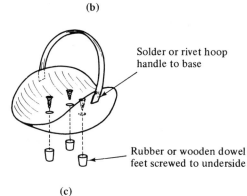

Solder or rivet hoop
handle to base

Rubber or wooden dowel
feet screwed to underside

(c)

appendix

Table A-1
DECIMAL EQUIVALENTS
OF FRACTIONS

Fraction	Decimal	Fraction	Decimal
$\frac{1}{64}$	0.015625	$\frac{33}{64}$	0.515625
$\frac{1}{32}$	0.03125	$\frac{17}{32}$	0.53125
$\frac{3}{64}$	0.046875	$\frac{35}{64}$	0.546875
$\frac{1}{16}$	0.0625	$\frac{9}{16}$	0.5625
$\frac{5}{64}$	0.078125	$\frac{37}{64}$	0.578125
$\frac{3}{32}$	0.09375	$\frac{19}{32}$	0.59375
$\frac{7}{64}$	0.109375	$\frac{39}{64}$	0.609375
$\frac{1}{8}$	0.125	$\frac{5}{8}$	0.625
$\frac{9}{64}$	0.140625	$\frac{41}{64}$	0.640525
$\frac{5}{32}$	0.15625	$\frac{21}{32}$	0.65625
$\frac{11}{64}$	0.171875	$\frac{43}{64}$	0.671875
$\frac{3}{16}$	0.1875	$\frac{11}{16}$	0.6875
$\frac{13}{64}$	0.203125	$\frac{45}{64}$	0.703125
$\frac{7}{32}$	0.21875	$\frac{23}{32}$	0.71875
$\frac{15}{64}$	0.234375	$\frac{47}{64}$	0.734375
$\frac{1}{4}$	0.250	$\frac{3}{4}$	0.750
$\frac{17}{64}$	0.265625	$\frac{49}{64}$	0.765625
$\frac{9}{32}$	0.28125	$\frac{25}{32}$	0.78125
$\frac{19}{64}$	0.296875	$\frac{51}{64}$	0.796875
$\frac{5}{16}$	0.3125	$\frac{13}{16}$	0.8125
$\frac{21}{64}$	0.328125	$\frac{53}{64}$	0.828125
$\frac{11}{32}$	0.34375	$\frac{27}{32}$	0.84375
$\frac{23}{64}$	0.359375	$\frac{55}{64}$	0.859375
$\frac{3}{8}$	0.375	$\frac{7}{8}$	0.875
$\frac{25}{64}$	0.390625	$\frac{57}{64}$	0.890625
$\frac{13}{32}$	0.40625	$\frac{29}{32}$	0.90625
$\frac{27}{64}$	0.421875	$\frac{59}{64}$	0.921875
$\frac{7}{16}$	0.4375	$\frac{15}{16}$	0.9375
$\frac{29}{64}$	0.453125	$\frac{61}{64}$	0.953125
$\frac{15}{32}$	0.46875	$\frac{31}{32}$	0.96875
$\frac{31}{64}$	0.484375	$\frac{63}{64}$	0.984375
$\frac{1}{2}$	0.500	1	1.000

Table A-2
ENGLISH
WEIGHTS AND MEASURES

Measures of Length

1 mile = 1760 yards = 5280 feet.

1 yard = 3 feet = 36 inches.   1 foot = 12 inches.

1 mil = 0.001 inch.   1 fathom = 2 yards = 6 feet.

1 rod = 5.5 yards = 16.5 feet.   1 hand = 4 inches.   1 span = 9 inches

1 micro-inch = one millionth inch or 0.000001 inch. (1 micrometer or micron = one millionth meter = 0.00003937 inch.)

Square Measure

1 square mile = 640 acres = 6400 square chains.

1 acre = 10 square chains = 4840 square yards = 43,560 square feet.

1 square chain = 16 square rods = 484 square yards = 4356 square feet.

1 square rod = 30.25 square yards = 272.25 square feet = 625 square links.

1 square yard = 9 square feet.

1 square foot = 144 square inches.

An acre is equal to a square, the side of which is 208.7 feet.

Measure used for Diameters and Areas of Electric Wires

1 circular inch = area of circle 1 inch in diameter = 0.7854 square inch.

1 circular inch = 1,000,000 circular mils.

1 square inch = 1.2732 circular inch = 1,273,239 circular mils.

A circular mil is the area of a circle 0.001 inch in diameter.

Cubic Measure

1 cubic yard = 27 cubic feet.

1 cubic foot = 1728 cubic inches.

The following measures are also used for wood and masonry:

1 cord of wood = 4 × 4 × 8 feet = 128 cubic feet.

1 perch of masonry = 16½ × 1½ × 1 foot = 24¾ cubic feet.

Table A-2—Cont.
ENGLISH
WEIGHTS AND MEASURES

Dry Measure

1 bushel (U. S. or Winchester struck bushel) = 1.2445 cubic foot = 2150.42 cubic inches.

1 bushel = 4 pecks = 32 quarts = 64 pints.

1 peck = 8 quarts = 16 pints.

1 quart = 2 pints.

1 heaped bushel = 1¼ struck bushel.

1 cubic foot = 0.8036 struck bushel.

1 British Imperial bushel = 8 Imperial gallons = 1.2837 cubic foot = 2218.19 cubic inches.

Liquid Measure

1 U. S. gallon = 0.1337 cubic foot = 231 cubic inches = 4 quarts = 8 pints.

1 quart = 2 pints = 8 gills.

1 pint = 4 gills.

1 British Imperial gallon = 1.2009 U. S. gallon = 277.42 cubic inches.

1 cubic foot = 7.48 U. S. gallons.

Apothecaries' Fluid Measure

1 U. S. fluid ounce = 8 drachms = 1.805 cubic inch = $\frac{1}{128}$ U. S. gallon.

1 fluid drachm = 60 minims.

1 British fluid ounce = 1.732 cubic inch.

Avoirdupois or Commercial Weight

1 gross or long ton = 2240 pounds.

1 net or short ton = 2000 pounds.

1 pound = 16 ounces = 7000 grains.

1 ounce = 16 drachms = 437.5 grains.

The following measures for weight are now seldom used in the United States:

1 hundred-weight = 4 quarters = 112 pounds (1 gross or long ton = 20 hundred-weights); 1 quarter = 28 pounds; 1 stone = 14 pounds; 1 quintal = 100 pounds.

Troy Weight, used for Weighing Gold and Silver

1 pound = 12 ounces = 5760 grains.
1 ounce = 20 pennyweights = 480 grains.
1 pennyweight = 24 grains.
1 carat (used in weighing diamonds) = 3.086 grains.
1 grain Troy = 1 grain avoirdupois = 1 grain apothecaries' weight.

Table A-3
METRIC WEIGHTS AND MEASURES

Measures of Length

10 millimeters (mm)	= 1 centimeter (cm).
10 centimeters	= 1 decimeter (dm).
10 decimeters	= 1 meter (m).
1000 meters	= 1 kilometer (km).

Square Measure

100 square millimeters (mm^2)	= 1 square centimeter (cm^2).
100 square centimeters	= 1 square decimeter (dm^2).
100 square decimeters	= 1 square meter (m^2).

Surveyor's Square Measure

100 square meters (m^2)	= 1 are (a).
100 ares	= 1 hectare (ha).
100 hectares	= 1 square kilometer (km^2).

Cubic Measure

1000 cubic millimeters (mm^3)	= 1 cubic centimeter (cm^3).
1000 cubic centimeters	= 1 cubic decimeter (dm^3).
1000 cubic decimeters	= 1 cubic meter (m^3).

Dry and Liquid Measure

10 milliliters (ml)	= 1 centiliter (cl).
10 centiliters	= 1 deciliter (dl).
10 deciliters	= 1 liter (l).
100 liters	= 1 hectoliter (hl).

1 liter = 1 cubic decimeter = the volume of 1 kilogram of pure water at a temperature of 39.2 degrees F.

Table A-3—Cont.
METRIC WEIGHTS AND MEASURES

Measures of Weight

10 milligrams (mg).	= 1 centigram (cg).
10 centigrams	= 1 decigram (dg).
10 decigrams	= 1 gram (g).
10 grams	= 1 dekagram (dag).
10 dekagrams	= 1 hectogram (hg).
10 hectograms	= 1 kilogram (kg).
1000 kilograms	= 1 (metric) ton (t).

Table A-4
METRIC AND ENGLISH
CONVERSION TABLE

Linear Measure

1 kilometer = 0.6214 mile.

1 meter = { 39.37 inches. / 3.2808 feet. / 1.0936 yards.

1 centimeter = 0.3937 inch.

1 millimeter = 0.03937 inch.

1 mile = 1.609 kilometers.

1 yard = 0.9144 meter.

1 foot = 0.3048 meter.

1 foot = 304.8 millimeters.

1 inch = 2.54 centimeters.

1 inch = 25.4 millimeters.

Square Measure

1 square kilometer = 0.3861 square mile = 247.1 acres.

1 hectare = 2.471 acres = 107,639 square feet.

1 are = 0.0247 acre = 1076.4 square feet.

1 square meter = 10.764 square feet = 1. 196 square yards.

1 square centimeter = 0.155 square inch.

1 square millimeter = 0.00155 square inch.

1 square mile = 2.5899 square kilometers.

1 acre = 0.4047 hectare = 40.47 ares.

1 square yard = 0.836 square meter.

1 square foot = 0.0929 square meter = 929 square centimeters.

1 square inch = 6.452 square centimeters = 645.2 square millimeters.

Cubic Measure

1 cubic meter = 35.315 cubic feet = 1.308 cubic yards.
1 cubic meter = 264.2 U. S. gallons.
1 cubic centimeter = 0.061 cubic inch.
1 liter (cubic decimeter) = 0.0353 cubic foot = 61.023 cubic inches.
1 liter = 0.2642 U. S. gallon = 1.0567 U. S. quarts.

1 cubic yard = 0.7646 cubic meter.
1 cubic foot = 0.02832 cubic meter = 28.317 liters.
1 cubic inch = 16.38706 cubic centimeters.
1 U. S. gallon = 3.785 liters.
1 U. S. quart = 0.946 liter.

Weight

1 metric ton = 0.9842 ton (of 2240 pounds) = 2204.6 pounds.
1 kilogram = 2.2046 pounds = 35.274 ounces avoirdupois.
1 gram = 0.03215 ounce troy = 0.03527 ounce avoirdupois.
1 gram = 15.432 grains.

1 ton (of 2240 pounds) = 1.016 metric ton = 1016 kilograms.
1 pound = 0.4536 kilogram = 453.6 grams.
1 ounce avoirdupois = 28.35 grams.
1 ounce troy = 31.103 grams.
1 grain = 0.0648 gram.
1 kilogram per square millimeter = 1422.32 pounds per square inch
1 kilogram per square centimeter = 14.223 pounds per square inch.
1 kilogram-meter = 7.233 foot-pounds.
1 pound per square inch = 0.0703 kilogram per square centimeter.
1 calorie (kilogram calorie) = 3.968 B.T.U. (British thermal unit).

index